WEAK ENOUGH TO LEAD

JAMES C. HOWELL

WEAK ENOUGH TO LEAD

What the Bible Tells Us
about Powerful Leadership

Abingdon Press®
Nashville

WEAK ENOUGH TO LEAD:
WHAT THE BIBLE TELLS US ABOUT POWERFUL LEADERSHIP

This book is printed on acid-free paper.

Library of Congress Cataloging-in-Publication Data has been requested.

ISBN: 978-1-5018-4263-4

17 18 19 20 21 22 23 24 25 26—10 9 8 7 6 5 4 3 2 1
MANUFACTURED IN THE UNITED STATES OF AMERICA

God chose me because I was weak enough. God does not do his great works by large committees. He trains somebody to be quiet enough, and little enough, and then he uses him.

—Hudson Taylor, missionary to China, 1894

I'm not interested in doing a good job. I am interested in an ecclesial vision for community. We are brothers and sisters, and Jesus is calling us from the pyramid to become a body.

—Jean Vanier, founder of L'Arche

CONTENTS

ix   Introduction: The Prayer of Jehoshaphat

1   Jesus: A Little Child Shall Lead Them

11   Hannah: Listening, and Letting Go

17   Saul: Tragically Flawed

26   David: The Natural

42   Kings and a Queen: Failures and Providence

50   Elijah: Loneliness and Renewal

60   Elisha: Mentoring and Humility

65   Micaiah: Yes-Men versus Truth-Tellers

69   Jeremiah: Courage and Its Costs

75   Amos, Second Isaiah: Judgment and Redemption

81   Genesis: Responsibility and Big Plans

88   Moses: Called, but Frustrated

101   Joshua and Samson: Commitment and Burnout

104   Priests: Thinking and Acting Institutionally

114   Sages: Elusive Wisdom

122   Peter and Paul: Downward Mobility

130   Epilogue: How Weakness Helps

133   Notes

145   Index of Names

INTRODUCTION

THE PRAYER OF JEHOSHAPHAT

A friend of mine was under consideration to become the senior pastor of a megachurch. He told me the best question anyone had asked him was, "Are you weak enough for this job?" Indeed. Everyone else was asking about qualifications, preaching ability, strategic vision, managerial savvy, and every other imaginable strength. But was he weak enough? Do we know our limitations; our inabilities; our fallen, vulnerable, broken selves? Is it that God uses our strengths? Or is it even truer that God's strength is perfected in our weakness (2 Cor 12:9)? If Jesus, our leader, was strong, then his was a strange and paradoxical kind of strength, as we will see.

For a long time I have been trying to make sense of the Bible while I've been leading—in the churches I've pastored and with the seminary students I've taught, but also in the city where I live, in my denomination and, most important of all, at home. I've listened to parents and businesspeople trying to lead in faithful ways. Jonathan Sacks is right: "We are all called on to be leaders within our sphere of influence, be it the family, the community, at work among colleagues or in play among teammates."[1] For him, a leader is the one who "lights a light while others curse the darkness."[2]

If God's "word is a lamp to my feet, / and a light to my path" (Ps 119:105), what do we see in the pages of the Bible that can illuminate and invigorate the leading we do? If we are hoping to glean a laundry list of "leadership principles" from the Bible, we will be sorely disappointed. What we find instead are real-life stories of gifted but limited people, all terribly flawed, trying to lead, struggling to connect well with those around them—not to mention the ways God can get involved in unwanted ways or just seem absent. Immersion in the tales of Saul, Hannah, Moses, Esther, Paul, and Jeremiah will leave you as challenged, exhausted, but renewed as Jacob after a long night of wrestling with a stranger—or was it with himself, or with God (Gen 32:22-32)?

How very different from the vast literature and cottage industry of workshops and videos on leadership available out in the world! When I was preparing to teach a class on leadership in seminary for the first time, I finally got around to all those business leadership books I had meant to read for years. As someone who has led large, complex organizations, I expected to be enthralled. Instead I felt ambivalence. The secular, business leadership gurus certainly offered lots of great ideas, and in the context of real corporate case studies. I took notes and put some of what I read into practice.

Yet at the same time it all seemed a little thin, too easy, and maybe failing to engage the profound complexities of human nature, inner darkness, historical forces, family dynamics, and sheer bad luck (or good luck). Besides, we might pick up a leadership book with the dream that reading it will dramatically increase success, productivity, or profit. But the Bible's vision for life and flourishing is pretty different from Wall Street's. Jesus as CEO? He'd run your company into the ground in a week. That notion he had about paying the guys who worked one hour the same full day's wage as those who'd put in twelve? The image of a farmer tossing precious seed onto a rocky path? Jesus would hire people who put "meekness" on their resume. The mere suggestion of "treasure on earth" got him rankled.

The Old Testament characters we will examine in this book would do no better. The kings of ancient Israel under whom the economy boomed, territory expanded, and the military was strong? You've never heard of them. Omri? Jeroboam II? Solomon you've heard of but, even though he ran the country swimmingly well, he was summarily judged as a failure, as were Omri and Jeroboam II. Prophetic leaders like Elijah and Jeremiah had few followers and wound up hounded and impoverished, or even imprisoned.

The very term *leadership*, when we analyze the Bible, is a bit of a misnomer. Biblical Hebrew has no words we can even translate as *leader* or *leadership*. In his magisterial *Old Testament Theology*, John Goldingay points out that in Israel, you only have "servants," not "leaders." Placing some people in authority over others is nothing but "a condescension to human sinfulness.... Leadership exists only because of sin."[3] So-called leaders in Israel seem to sin more than regular people "because they have opportunity to sin in more spectacular ways."[4]

And yet God is all about condescension to human sinfulness. When leading happened well, it was from a nameless sage who taught wisely in a small hamlet, a similarly nameless priest who faithfully guided people through sacrifice and healing, a mother who organized families in the community to care for a random Moabite who had made his way into their village. Some prophets told the truth. A few kings ruled humbly and faithfully—yet never in ways that would work effectively in today's corporate world and might even seem strange and even contradictory in today's church and world. Paul was weak and bragged about it. Jesus, the greatest leader ever, led the very few who hung on until the end where he would lead us: to the cross.

Life Stories, not Principles

Although the Bible yields no "leadership principles," it is full of stories, which is how leadership actually happens. Even in our world, leadership that is great or disastrous or at least interesting is never about a blueprint of principles being enacted one after another. There's always a story, involving some luck, unexpected twists and turns, a random phone call that changed everything, an illness that interrupted the schedule for weeks, personal trouble at home, a late-night cocktail leading to moral failure, an election that caused policy changes, and more luck both good and bad. My life is like the life of Bible people. I am not seven propositions or ten principles. I am a guy who grew up in a dysfunctional family and have been blessed and severely challenged, with a lot of luck and chance, by all manner of folks and God's involvement all woven together.

And as God created each one of us as unique as a snowflake or a fingerprint, so every leader will be special in the ways he or she succeeds and falters. The *Harvard Business Review* tried to explain "why more than 1000 studies have not produced a profile of an ideal leader."[5] The answer, for all those interesting and exemplary leaders, is that "their leadership emerged from their life stories."[6] Our life stories, just like the life stories of the characters in the Bible, do not provide tidy answers to questions. Our stories raise more questions than they answer. How lucky are we, that even in the realm of leadership, the question asked is always infinitely more valuable than the answer given.

Secular leadership experts are coming to understand this. Ronald Heifetz, in his aptly titled book, *Leadership Without Easy Answers*, describes the quest for the wrong kind of leadership: "We call for someone with answers, decision, strength...someone who can make hard problems simple....Instead of looking for saviors, we should be calling for leadership that will challenge us to face problems for which there are no simple, painless solutions."[7]

As this book will demonstrate, we find no simple, painless answers in scripture to questions of leadership.

Elaine Heath has made the intriguing suggestion that the church, finding itself in something of a "dark night of the soul," is in trouble—"the kind of trouble that requires leadership from those who are holy."[8] I might add "humble, vulnerable, merciful, prayerful, weak, desperate," and a few other adjectives, which really flesh out what holiness looked like in Bible times and what leadership could be today. What we need are leaders deeply immersed in the scriptures. The overarching plot of the story of whatever leadership was in the Bible is that hope resides not in human ability or clever programs but in the love of God, which is relentless and refuses to let God's purpose fall to the ground.

The Prayer of Jehoshaphat

My favorite biblical prayer, when I think about leadership, is tucked away in an obscure chapter of 2 Chronicles. King Jehoshaphat was about to lead Israel into battle. In the most unleaderlike way conceivable, he prayed to the Lord, out loud so everyone could hear: "We do not know what to do, but our eyes are on you" (2 Chr 20:12).

The Moabites and Ammonites were nipping at Jerusalem's heels, having encroached all the way to En-Gedi. The people, the soldiers, the old men, wives, widows, and children, fearful, hopeful, and in dire need of leadership, flocked to Jehoshaphat. But what did they find? "Jehoshaphat was afraid" (2 Chr 20:3). How did they know? What did they see? A jittery hand? A blanched complexion? Perspiration beads on the forehead? Edwin Friedman was surely right when he wrote of "the benefits of being a nonanxious presence" and that the capacity of leaders to contain their own anxiety "may be the most significant capability in their arsenal."[9] Jehoshaphat was palpably anxious. He proclaimed a fast and then offered up his prayer to the Lord: "We do not know what to do, but our eyes are on you."

Perhaps, like me, you've been in seminars or at lunch with a band of self-confident, highly successful leaders, who seem to know exactly what to do. It seems downright magical, so doable, so profitable. Just apply the hedgehog concept or Drucker's principles, make the right contact over cocktails, put in the long hours and everything will sizzle! In such settings, I feel a twinge of envy. I make some notes in my head, but generally I just feel a bit small, too hesitant, a tad dim-witted about subtle political complexities.

Jehoshaphat's prayer provides some solace. From the Bible's perspective, uncertainty, weakness, and inability aren't necessarily problems to be coped with or eventually fixed. God did not create us to be superhuman. Weakness is just who and what we are. God created us with limitations—and they are designed for our benefit! As a preacher, I've always loved what Karl Barth explained so well: "We ought to speak of God. We are human, however, and so cannot speak of God. We ought therefore to recognize both our obligation and our inability and by that very recognition give God the glory. This is our perplexity."[10]

Leaders ought to lead well. But we are human, however, so we cannot, or only falteringly. So could it be that in our obligation to lead, and then in our inability to lead, we give God the glory?

Some nonreligious teachers of leadership are naming the gifts of weakness and limitation that the Bible laid out in the open centuries ago. Brené Brown and Patrick Lencioni are two who have explained how leaders can and must be vulnerable, and quite open about their weaknesses, in order to build trust within working teams.[11] We only lead as broken, flawed, incapable people, and we lead people who need to get over their fantasies that we will have all the answers when we do not. The best favor we can offer them may be to stand up like Jehoshaphat. They will notice the trembling knees and sweaty palms. And then we lead with the only sensible prayer possible: "We do not know what to do, but our eyes are on you."

Mind you, Jehoshaphat's story has a bit of a pastel, cardboard, fairytale-like ending. The army, instead of marching out with weapons, simply sang hymns. God swooped down and Israel's enemies were routed. Were it so simple. Leadership in the real world can begin with Jehoshaphat's eloquent prayer. But it continues in difficulty. Thankfully, the majority of the Bible's stories about leadership are complicated. Mistakes are made. Motives are mixed. Confusion reigns. Holiness and hostility pop out of the very same person and on the same day. Family dynamics confound leadership. Gifts are utilized and squandered. Fate and circumstance play their roles. And God's hand is in it all—not orchestrating everything to turn out smoothly but being present, transforming in hidden ways, bringing things to God's good end, although the good is far from obvious. That's what we are really seeking in the first place: not a few tips we can implement with flair but the merciful, holy presence of the living God.

Study Questions

1. How do you feel about the question, "Are you weak enough to lead?"

2. In what sphere or spheres of influence can you lead? Do you light a light or curse the darkness?

3. What has unfolded in your life's story to make you the person you are?

4. What do you think about Jehoshaphat's prayer?

JESUS

A Little Child Shall Lead Them

E ven though the words may feel familiar because we've heard them so many times, what could be more curious, and less promising, than Isaiah's prophecy, "And a little child shall lead them" (Isa 11:6)? When God came to save God's people, to lead them from their lonely exile into the promised salvation, God came as a child. Any Christian who would lead, at work, at home, in the community, at church, wherever, has to sort out this puzzle that our leader is (or was) a child.

We could say Jesus *was* a child, in the same way that we consider childhood to be just a temporary stage along the way to adulthood. We might envision Jesus as some kind of wonder-child, a phenom, a one-in-a-zillion prodigy. Some of those early apocryphal Gospels depicted Jesus in his playpen, molding clay into birds before miraculously causing them to fly, or striking dead some boys who bullied him on the playground. Byzantine art depicted the infant Jesus as a miniature potentate, dressed in regal attire, with the stern gaze of a ruler, while sitting on his mother's lap.

But the point of the incarnation is that Jesus was a child like other children. Jesus, our leader, was led by his mother. When she told him *Let's go to the market* or *It's time for bed* or *Let's recite Psalm 8 together* he followed. He was entirely and wonderfully dependent upon her. She nursed him, and rocked him when he cried out from a fever. She

1

prepared all his food. She made and mended all his clothes. She taught him how to talk and how to pray. She delighted in his first steps and comforted him when he fell and scraped his knee. Every leader begins in such humility, for which we can be grateful. I'm not self-made. Someone loved me and was tender toward me. I've been totally dependent, and will be again someday—and am now, if I'm attentive to things.

We could invert what we just said, though, and say Jesus led his mother. As a weak, helpless, fledgling child, he led her precisely by being weak. His immobility was her cue to carry him. His hunger invited her to feed him. His cries were the kinds of commands every mother obeys—by holding, weeping, whispering soothing words. We know that at the cross, and after the church was born, Mary continued in her life vocation as the first and best follower of her child.

Recall the last time you saw a small child brought into a room of people. Everything changed. The weak one has the power to elicit tenderness and cooing or to make folks upset and ask for the child to be removed. As his hysterical, violent reaction demonstrated, King Herod intuitively understood that his royal standing was indeed threatened by the birth of a vulnerable child.

Our only glimpses of Jesus's childhood are provided by Luke. First there is the happy summary in 2:52: "And Jesus increased in wisdom and stature, and in favor with God and man" (KJV). The infant, the child, the teenage Jesus was not omniscient; he was a learner, and he grew wiser over the years. We pray that wisdom and favor continue to grow, always, for all of us, well past the time we grow physically taller.

The other is that harrowing moment when Mary and Joseph realized their twelve-year-old boy was missing—and it took three days to find him! Of course (or so he assumed they'd know), he was in the temple. We overrate the scene if we visualize him as a boy genius, a prodigy teaching the teachers. Rather wonderfully, but not at all abnormally, Jesus was "sitting among the teachers, listening to them and asking them questions" (Luke 2:46). Jesus exhibited that lovely weakness we call *curiosity*: the weakness that doesn't have all that much figured out just yet, the weakness of asking instead of assuming or telling, the weakness of stammering awe before mystery and wonder. The child Jesus, as our leader, has shown us the way in corporate church and communal life by being weak enough to be puzzled and ask lots of questions. The art of all leadership begins and ends with the asking of good questions.

Becoming Like Children

Isaiah's idea that "a little child shall lead them" had to have resonated deeply with Jesus after he was grown up. When his disciples shushed children and tried to usher them away, Jesus welcomed them: "Let the little children come to me" (Matt 19:14). How kind of Jesus! But then he added, "It is to such as these that the kingdom of heaven belongs" (v. 14). Children aren't just part of the kingdom. It belongs to them.

Earlier, in a startling moment, Jesus had said to the grownups, "Unless you change and become like children, you will never enter the kingdom of heaven" (Matt 18:3). We can't be sure what all he had in mind. Children are innocent. Their jaws drop in awe over little things. They don't hide their treasures; they share their toys. They don't fret over tomorrow. Children toddle and fall down a lot. They require much mercy. They know how to play, and waste time. Children are under no illusion that they are independent. They are entirely dependent and seem happy about it. God yearns for all these naïve, holy dispositions to be restored in us.

The core of childlikeness is that children are small and weak. In a world that demands that we be strong, Jesus oddly but hopefully invites us into weakness. Hans Urs von Balthasar pointed out that "only the Christian religion, which in its essence is communicated by the eternal child of God, keeps alive in its believers the lifelong awareness of their being children, and therefore of having to ask and give thanks for things."[1]

But we shouldn't idealize childhood as we reflect on Jesus asking us to become like children. Children are demanding. Children argue and whine. Martin Luther, stressed by his rambunctious household of six children aged four to twelve, puzzled over this idea of becoming like children: "What was Jesus thinking? This is too much: must we become such idiots?"[2]

Jesus's Leadership Principles

If we think at all carefully about Jesus as our model for leadership, we will wonder what kinds of idiots Jesus might want us to be. Although some have spoken of "Jesus's leadership principles," or imagined Jesus as a CEO or even the president, putting Jesus in charge of an institution would be like asking a four-year-old to run the place or an eight-year-old to fly a plane or a six-year-old to hold the keys to the bank. Imagine corporate policies like "Turn the other cheek," "Do not store up treasure on earth," "Take no gold or bag on your journey," or "Sell all you have and give to the poor." Jesus approached fairly successful businessmen, fishermen, and tax collectors, and talked them into leaving it all behind to wander around the countryside and risk life and limb. Jesus's best story was of a father who threw a big party for the son who had squandered half the family business in riotous living.

We might wonder what kind of review Jesus would write of Jim Collins's best-selling leadership book, *From Good to Great*. One of Collins's cardinal principles is getting the right people on the bus and getting the wrong people off the bus. He's absolutely right—and yet Jesus seemed determined to keep everybody, especially the wrong people, on the bus. We who are church leaders struggle so agonizingly when we need to fire someone—and if Jesus is our leader, then actually we should struggle, since his life-and-death mission was to prove that every person is redeemable.

Jesus, of all people, knew God's rules in scripture. But he would defy one of God's own rules in a heartbeat in order to help someone who was hurting. He healed on the Sabbath, touched untouchables, and intervened to prevent a lawbreaker from being stoned. Danny Meyer, the renowned restaurateur in New York, has explained that his business is all about hospitality. Yes, there are policies. But "policies are nothing more than guidelines to be broken for the benefit of our guests."[3]

His employees are instructed to be "agents," not "gatekeepers." If asked, "Can I make a reservation for two at seven?" a gatekeeper responds, "No, we're full." The agent says, "Let me check" or "Let me see if I can shift someone around" or "Let me contact the restaurant next door for you." It's hospitality when people feel something is done *for* them not when things happen *to* them. Jesus, who figured out how to feed everybody (strangers, the uninvited, and even his enemies), would be the greatest restaurant manager in history.

Most business leaders understand that leadership is about hospitality. Followers of Jesus are prepared to take this to any extreme. He taught us to love our enemies, to welcome strangers, to touch those who seem disgusting. When it comes to the outsider, or the one who is different, Jesus would concur with the intriguing idea that hospitality is curiosity. I want to welcome the other because I'm interested. Or maybe hospitality is courageous: Jesus's model for hospitality would be the Germans who hid Jews in their homes during World War II or foster parents who happily adopt the most challenging of children.

Payday in Jesus's Vineyard

Jesus made up a shocking story about a vineyard owner who hired laborers in the morning, hired some more later in the day, hired still more in the afternoon, and finally hired a few with only an hour left in the day. When the laborers lined up for their pay, he gave every last one of them a denarius. Quite fair—for a full day's work. Not surprisingly, the guys who put in more time were furious. We are tempted to put some clever spin on the story, as if it is about late-in-life conversion, or even the magnificent bounty of God's saving grace.

But Amy-Jill Levine, rightly pointing out that "Jesus was more interested in how we love our neighbor than how we get into heaven," asks an intriguing question: "Might we rather see the parable as about real workers in a real marketplace and real landowners who hire those workers?"[4] Our gut reaction is *No way!* But wasn't Jesus the kind of guy who wanted everyone to have enough? If the guys who were hired late, through no fault of their own, only got one-twelfth of a day's wage, their families would starve. This is the same Jesus who told a rich man to sell everything, who directed party hosts to invite those who couldn't invite them in return, who spoke of lenders forgiving massive financial debts, who included despised and untouchable people in his close circle, who visited Zaccheus and left him so staggered he gave his hard-earned money back with interest to those he'd earned it from.

Shares of stock in a company run by Jesus would plummet in value. But he is our leader, the childlike one who never tired of asking hard questions. Could we, his followers, lead in very different ways, in weaker ways? Clarence Jordan, founder of Koinonia Farms and creator of the *Cotton Patch Gospel*, was a bold, no-holds-barred Christian, one of those once-in-a-generation believers radical enough to dare to do what's in the Bible. One Sunday he preached at a gilded, high steeple church in Atlanta. After the service, the pastor asked him for some advice. The church custodian had eight children and earned a mere eighty dollars per week. The concerned minister claimed he tried to get the man a raise but with no success. Jordan considered this for a minute, and then said, "Why don't you just swap salaries with the janitor? That wouldn't require any extra money in the budget."[5]

Jesus was like the child who can't stop asking questions, like the child who sees a homeless person by the road and asks *Mommy, can't he live at our house?* Maybe a leader can't pull off the vineyard wage maneuver or even the salary swap. But is there a way to lean in that direction, to engage in something dramatic, to veer a bit more toward Jesus than business as usual? Jesus asks leaders not merely to obey the law or even to be kind, but to be different.

After all, Jesus started his first sermon by saying, "Blessed are the poor in spirit....Blessed are the meek....Blessed are the merciful....[And] blessed are the pure in heart" (Matt 5:3-8). We can be sure Jesus didn't mean *This applies out here on this mountain or at church or in your private life but not in the real world.* What if we honored meekness and mercy when we are leading? What if we looked for and celebrated business leaders and even politicians who are meek, and pure in heart? Instead of rallying around tough, cynical, pragmatic, get-it-done-at-all-costs leaders, we might seek out those who know their weaknesses, who are humble and holy. Of course there is a steep price to pay for being like Jesus. It cost Jesus, our leader, his life. Clarence Jordan was firebombed by the Ku Klux Klan. Francis of Assisi, who led thousands of friars by simply acting like Jesus, giving away possessions and embracing the untouchables, was sued and imprisoned by his own father.

Binding the Strong Man

But we must always remember what is at stake: not this business or that church or a single family. There is a cosmic battle going on. Jesus had shown from the moment he walked onto the stage of history that his real foe wasn't hunger or sickness or a lack of faith but the devil, evil itself. Jesus spoke not of himself but someone else—Satan!—as "the strong man" (Mark 3:27); Jesus's mission was to bind him. Jesus's strategy to bind this strong man? Not muscle or miracles. The devil pounced on Jesus in the wilderness, finding him in a much-weakened state after six weeks of not eating. He taunted Jesus, reminding him that Jesus had the strength to turn stones into bread and to leap safely from the pinnacle of the temple. Jesus even had the very real opportunity to rule all the kingdoms on earth. But Jesus chose to be weak, to forego the food and fanfare. He let the kingdoms rule themselves, fully realizing one of them would kill him in the end.

We may think Jesus was play-acting: the super strong one barely restraining himself, trying weakness on for a little while to make a point before resuming his titanic power. But maybe, in his deepest self, Jesus really was weak, not in the sense of being flawed but in the sense of not being mighty. Jesus was the first to understand fully the problem with power. The powerful can achieve a great many things. But power cannot be loved. Power stirs fear. Jesus told us not to be afraid; he would settle for nothing less than tender love.

Jesus certainly had his moments when he exhibited downright superhuman strength. He stilled a storm. He fed thousands. He cured lepers. But then he turned around and hushed those who wanted to tell everybody how strong he was: "He sternly ordered them not to make him known" (Mark 3:12). Was he afraid they would misunderstand his true mission, fawn over his wonderworking and demand constant displays of power?

There was a dramatic shift in the plot of Jesus's life midstream. After a season of strength, where he spoke powerfully and dazzled with miracles, he turned toward Jerusalem. In the second half of each Gospel, there are virtually no miracles. Jesus increasingly became passive—someone acted upon. He was "handed over" to the Roman authorities and the Sadducees by Judas. He said nothing when tried by Pontius Pilate, who scoffed over the foolish notion that one so weak could be a king.

Without lifting a finger in his own defense, Jesus passively and dependently let himself be nailed up on a shaft of wood. Humiliated, mocked, so weak he lost his followers, he hung there helplessly. His mother, Mary, who had given him his lifeblood, who had held him when he was helpless as an infant, looked on her child, shattered. Children learn to sing, "Little ones to him belong; they are weak, but he is strong."[6] But if we ponder the climax of Jesus's story, we might change the lyrics to "They are weak, and he is too."

Where Jesus Leads

Jesus our leader leads us to one place: the cross. This is the truth about Jesus. This is his glory—not the miracles or the wise teachings. It is the completely weak, dead Jesus that prompts the centurion to confess, "Truly this man was God's Son!" (Mark 15:39). We hurry past Good Friday, preferring the pretty colors and sunny victory of Easter. But even the way the resurrection story is told underlines a kind of weakness: Jesus didn't vigorously shove the rock aside and stride boldly out of the tomb, knocking the soldiers aside. The verbs are all passive: Jesus was raised.

Our most eloquent theologians have wrestled with this paradox, this dark, puzzling truth that is the shining, clarifying truth in God's own heart. Hans Urs von Balthasar asked who was responsible for Jesus's crucifixion: Was it the Romans or the Jews? Pilate? Herod? Caiaphas? Judas? The crowd? "He rolls like a ball between the competitors, thrown from one to another, held by none, undesired by all....No one wishes to be responsible. That is why they are all guilty."[7] If leadership is taking responsibility, then Jesus in his seeming passivity is the one taking responsibility for all the others—and for us.

Dietrich Bonhoeffer may have put it best in a letter he wrote to his friend Eberhard Bethge from the Tegel prison shortly before his own death: "God lets himself be pushed out of the world on to the cross. He is weak and powerless in the world, and that is precisely the way, the only way, in which he is with us and helps us."[8]

How could weakness and powerlessness possibly help? Why did Jesus choose this lowly, weak path? Why did Jesus tell his followers, even as he was giving them authority to lead his church, that they should take up *their* crosses and follow him? We will wrestle with these questions in the rest of this book. For now, we turn back the pages in the book that was Jesus's Bible to poke around in the Old Testament's stories of leaders, to see how strength and weakness unfolded for them, and to learn, just as Jesus did, from their struggles, family dysfunctions, wins and losses, strivings and failings, all under the auspices of God's mercy and will.

Study Questions

1. What is refreshing about the idea of children as leaders?

2. Who was the first person who led you as a child, and what was that like?

3. Imagine you just sat down in the restaurant Jesus owns. What would the experience be like?

4. If Jesus envisioned a radically different world where everyone has enough, should Christian leaders lead differently?

5. How can Jesus's weakness and powerlessness help?

HANNAH

Listening, and Letting Go

To explore leadership in the Old Testament, we should begin with Saul, Israel's first king, its first official leader of anything like an institution. His government had to have been a bit slapdash, a "startup"— understandably. Israel had no capital city, no buildings or officials as yet. Israel was nothing more than a loose confederation of extended families living precariously across an expanse of rugged territory they did not in any way control. When Saul assumed leadership, Israel was so small other nations would have chuckled to learn they now had a king. Israel could not have been weaker.

Who better than Saul to lead a small, weak, fledgling startup nation? He was big and strong. "There was not a man among the people of Israel more handsome than he; he stood head and shoulders above everyone else" (1 Sam 9:2). His father, Kish, was wealthy. In his first battle, Saul deployed his anxious troops brilliantly and crushed the Ammonites. His spiritual prowess was noteworthy: "The spirit of God possessed him, and he fell into a prophetic frenzy," leading onlookers to ask, "Is Saul also among the prophets?" (1 Sam 10:10, 12). Companies, churches, and organizations quite naturally look to those who seem impressive. But looks are deceiving. Saul had his tragic flaws. We might say he was too strong—certainly too strong to lead the people of the God who chooses and then uses the small and weak.

11

If we turn back a few pages, we discover the real dawn of a new day for Israel was not when Saul was crowned but when a woman, a nobody, unable to conceive, surprisingly gave birth to a son—as if the script for what would unfold for Mary and Jesus fluttered down to earth centuries earlier. Hannah was barren, which was the ultimate weakness for women in the Bronze Age. She had nothing going for her except the tender love of her husband, Elkanah. She was taunted by her rival, Peninnah, whose cruel words twisted like a knife in her gut.

Hannah did what the helpless do: "Hannah rose and presented herself before the LORD. . . . She was deeply distressed and prayed to the LORD, and wept bitterly" (1 Sam 1:9-10). Anguished prayer is weakness splayed all over the floor. Eli the priest observed her and assumed she was drunk. Then he took pity on her. Or perhaps he realized he was witnessing what every priest longs to see: a soul entirely abandoned to God. He blessed her. And then this woman, with no natural strength in her womb, conceived and bore a son, Samuel.

The Promise Kept

The mind-boggling wrinkle in Hannah's story, though, isn't the seemingly miraculous birth. What staggers us is that she kept an outlandish promise she had made in her desperation. Trying to coax God into giving her a child, she pledged to give that child right back to God. She could easily have reneged on the deal once she cradled her precious son in her arms, nursing him and giggling with glee over his arrival. He was all she'd ever wanted. And in those days, a son was your social security, the one a woman needed to care for her in old age.

But she took the boy to Shiloh and left him there to serve in the temple as an apprentice to Eli. What more poignant words are there in all of scripture than these? "She left him there for the LORD" (1 Sam 1:28). The world says *Grab the gifts you can, hang on to them, accumulate strength and resources.* But Hannah, instead of clinging tightly, opened her hands and let go of the best gift ever. She chose to return to her weak, vulnerable state. "She left him there for the LORD."

There is a kind of holy leading the world will never understand. After his election, Pope Francis handed back the powers of the papacy he'd just won by riding in a Ford Focus instead of the papal limousine, by moving into a guesthouse instead of the Apostolic Palace, and by wearing a simple cassock instead of regal finery. Henri Nouwen left a faculty position at Harvard to live in a L'Arche community in Canada, where his job was to care for a single, severely handicapped young man named Adam. Maybe the most effective pastor I've ever known declined multiple promotions, quietly mentored dozens of young clergy, and, in her parishes, happily beamed offstage as her laity excelled as they never had before.

Imagine all those obscure people who have led so marvelously that we have never heard of them. Leadership is letting go: a refusal of possession, control or manipulation, an offering to God. Letting go must be the secret to leadership, since it is the secret of all of life; the results are those immeasurables like contentment, gratitude, and the flourishing of others. I love Wendell Berry's novel about a Kentucky farm mother, Hannah Coulter, who muses,

> The chance you had in life is the life you've got. You can make complaints about what people, including you, make of their lives after they have got them, and about what people make of other people's lives, even about your children being gone, but you mustn't wish for another life. You mustn't want to be someone else. What you must do is this: "Rejoice evermore. Pray without ceasing. In everything give thanks." I am not all the way capable of so much, but those are the right instructions.[1]

Leaders let go of fantasies and selfish wishes, resentments and any sense of entitlement or deserving. How countercultural! Leaders can be content; we already have enough, and so we are freed for joy. Who wouldn't follow a leader to a place of joy?

Speak, Lord, Your Servant Is Listening

Hannah's little boy, Samuel, was to become one of Israel's great leaders and yet with heart-wrenching complications. Before we explore those, we should linger over the brief glimpse we get of his childhood. "The boy Samuel grew up in the presence of the LORD" (1 Sam 2:21). But all was not well in Shiloh, where a crisis in leadership had reached the boiling point. Eli was old, and his sons, under apprenticeship to succeed their father, "were scoundrels; they had no regard for the Lord or for the duties of the priests" (vv. 12-13). Their avarice, wickedness, and bullying were no secret, and they turned a deaf ear to their father's pleading.

How dumbfounding is this? Samuel grew up watching elderly Eli struggle to rein in his deplorable sons, and then, when Samuel himself was old, his own sons treated him and God in precisely the same way. Leadership books and consultants might help us draw up thoughtful succession plans. But can they ever account for the unpredictable effects of garden variety human sinfulness, even among those reared in holy environments and with the best possible parents or mentors?

The Bible's stories awaken us to a rarely acknowledged reality: so many leaders, while striving to implement unquestionably correct principles and strategies, are walking around with the hushed but crushing burden of children or other loved ones who are breaking their hearts. Might we be gentler with those who lead, suspecting they may well carry hidden griefs? Might I be the one trusted to listen, care, and not judge? Can I be gentle and patient with myself when I haul the horrific weight of family dysfunction into work or the church?

In the swirl of tension, chaos, and sorrow in Eli's household, young Samuel somehow managed "to grow both in stature and in favor with the LORD and with the people" (1 Sam 2:26). Although "the word of the LORD was rare in those days" (3:1), Samuel heard the Lord call him just after bedtime one night. "Samuel! Samuel!" He responded, "Here I am"—and ran to Eli. But it was not Eli who was calling him. (See vv. 4-8.) When this happened a third time, it dawned on Eli what was going on. His instruction was magnificent: "Go, lie down; and if he calls you, you shall say, 'Speak, Lord, for your servant is listening'" (v. 9).

And so he did, and the logjam broke open, and God's new thing began to unfold. It is easy, over-simplistic, and maybe just too pious to say *Leaders should pray.* Of course they should pray. But as is the case with most of our praying, we think prayer is when we ask God for favors, like *Help me lead well,* or *Help me with this decision,* or *Let this deal come through!* Samuel's prayer, learned from Eli, asked for nothing at all. He was simply quiet, receptive, ready to listen; he had what the great mystic writer Maggie Ross called "a willingness for whatever."[2] "Speak, Lord, for your servant is listening."

Of course, we make our plans, and we seek God's help. But wise leaders know their weakness: that their best-laid plans may well be out of sync with God's. "Oh, rebellious children... / who carry out a plan, but not mine" (Isa 30:1). Even when we listen, we humbly allow for the possibility we didn't hear God clearly, or at all. We are humble. We rely on mercy. We hope God will use even our missteps. We strive to fine-tune our receptivity to God. Faithful leadership begins and ends in growing, not the bottom line, or my reputation, but our ability to be absorbed in God's mind and ways.

Study Questions

1. Does hope for our world come from the visible and mighty people? Or from more obscure, humble, unknown people?

2. Why is the best leadership about giving up instead of gaining?

3. Should leaders be content?

4. Can we picture the private, unknown life of a leader who is frustrating others and have mercy?

5. What should leaders pray for? And how might we pray for them?

SAUL

Tragically Flawed

Listening to and following God seem simple with Hannah and young Samuel. More complicated by far, though, is the perplexing life of King Saul. He had become king after the clamoring of a nervous crowd led to his acclamation. The story of that momentous day, recounted in 1 Samuel 8, is the overture to the long, tragic, embarrassing and yet theologically hopeful story of kingship in Israel—and a case study in the complex realism of biblical leadership. "All the elders of Israel gathered together and came to Samuel at Ramah, and said to him, 'You are old' [a frank but unflattering opening remark] 'and your sons do not follow in your ways' [similarly frank and unflattering]; 'appoint for us, then, a king to govern us, like other nations.' But the thing displeased Samuel" (1 Sam 8:4-6).

Perhaps he was displeased that they were so frank and unflattering as to reject his sons. Was he clinging to hopes they would turn out all right after all? Did he seek some validation through them? Was he, in old age, shortsighted regarding what was required in such tough times? How did the author of 1 Samuel get this peek into Samuel's sentimental confusion? And how did he know Samuel's displeasure was shared by God—who if anything felt more jilted than did Samuel? "The LORD

said to Samuel...'They have rejected me from being king over them'"
(1 Sam 8:7).

The Refusal of Power

Why was their desire for a king unholy? After all, times were changing. Nation-states were forming all over the world. The Bronze Age was yielding to the Iron Age. Nomadic culture was yielding to increasing urbanization. Centralized power was the logical next step for the fledgling Israelites. Security demanded it.

But this was not the first time they had asked for a king. A few decades earlier the Lord raised up Gideon, who pulled off a stunning and downright miraculous military victory over the Midianites. His army, when they embarked, was simply too...strong? God instructed Gideon to keep merely three hundred of the thirty-two-thousand soldiers he started with. The weakened hand was not expected to win, but Gideon and the few trounced the Midianites. How to apply this to leadership today is elusive, but intriguing.

Understandably, and a little confused about how the victory happened, the tribes clamored around Gideon: "Rule over us, you and your son and your grandson also" (Judg 8:22). With immense humility and piety, at least as the story was retold by the author of Judges, Gideon replied, "I will not rule over you, and my son will not rule over you; the Lord will rule over you" (v. 23).

Gideon was the gold standard of biblical leadership. He refused any office or status. He performed the task God set before him, declared they were subject only to God, and then returned home. We might think of Cincinnatus or George Washington—or even Frodo Baggins from *The Lord of the Rings*: not seizing the ring of power, he accomplished his daunting task and then went home to the shire. We cannot know what the people thought about Gideon's refusal. But they clung to their wish for a king and fell for Abimelech, one of Gideon's many sons. His makeshift reign lasted just three years and ended in disaster.

When the people pressed Samuel for a king, had they forgotten Gideon and Abimelech? Was the notion of the Lord as king just feeling too flimsy? Piety was one thing, but the Midianites and Philistines wielded real swords and clubs. Israel was under siege—and in such times, the Bible's simple vision of trust in God didn't mesh well with the demands of real societies trying to adjust and survive. The Prussian chancellor Bismarck famously pointed out that the Sermon on the Mount isn't a good blueprint for leading a government. Leaders can't merely close their eyes, fold their hands in prayer, and refuse to get their hands dirty, can they?

God Gave Them Up

The sensible demand for Samuel to give them a king took a stunning turn when the Lord, nursing feelings of rejection, told Samuel, "Listen to the voice of the people in all that they say to you" (1 Sam 8:7). What they were asking was a bolt away from God toward independence, a surrender of their status as God's chosen, special, elect people. But instead of tossing down a few thunderbolts, God let them have what they wanted. Paul wrote in a similar vein in Romans 1: "God gave them up." When people insist on their will instead of God's, God "gives them up"; God lets them have their way.

And yet the resilience of God's love wouldn't let God just abandon them to their own devices. After telling Samuel to let them have their king, God simply added, "only—you shall solemnly warn them, and show them the ways of the king who shall reign over them" (1 Sam 8:9). A laundry list of troubles (all of which did eventually unfold in the sad narrative to come) was rattled off: "This king will press your sons into vain military quests, and your daughters into domestic service; he will tax you and confiscate the fruits of your labors."[1] But the people only hardened their hearts, shouting, "No! but we are determined to have a king over us, so that ... [he may] go out before us and fight our battles" (vv. 19-20). The key word here is *our*. Their agenda, not the Lord's. We

19

may wonder how many of the Bible's "holy wars" were really very human wars with God's name pasted on the outside. How hard is it for leaders who are pressured to do what they know is not of God?

A crucial responsibility of the leader is to warn, to see the big picture, and to notice where some hidden undertow might pull everybody under. When Samuel warned, what was his tone of voice? Did he snarl and bellow, raspy and loud, like a street preacher inveighing against the wind? Or was his tone gentler, more plaintive, a tender pleading? Love warns gingerly, lovingly. And yet our Bible stories serve as a sober reminder that in the face of warning most people only stiffen in their wrongheaded resolve. There is much frustration and grief in leadership. Fallen human nature will thwart our best efforts and expose the feebleness of simplistic leadership tips.

Perhaps things didn't have to go sour at this turning point in Israel's history. Tim Laniak makes an intriguing suggestion: "God is opposed to the *intent*—more than the *content*—of the request."[2] Could the people have asked differently? *Give us a king—but a special kind of king, a holy, humble king, unlike the kings of the other nations?* Or after the dire warnings, might they have listened and adjusted? *Give us a king, but let's build in safeguards, a balance of powers?* Behind the scenes, God did just this for them, as we will see.

If we step back and survey the centuries-long plot of the entire Bible, what we see is this: God said *No king*. The people insisted. God acceded. They suffered for it. But God wound up using this institution of kingship—by filling the throne with Jesus, God's own son. And then there was never a need for another king. God appears to have taken their misguided rebellion and used it to fulfill God's ultimate redemptive purpose.

Like a Greek Tragedy

But back to the Bronze Age: God let them have what they wanted. Oddly enough, the name *Saul* means "asked for." The rich irony of this!

The people ask for a king, and, after dire warnings, God gives them literally what they asked for: Saul, the asked-for one. Poor Saul. He was inserted into the middle of a fractured relationship between Israel and the Lord. He was immensely gifted, tall, strong, smart, and zealous. Maybe too zealous. We almost sense that he tried too hard. Leaders often do, especially in sick systems.

Saul could be the poster boy for the kind of failed leadership Ronald Heifetz and Marty Linsky pinpoint as the most common: facing "adaptive challenges," leaders treat them as if they were mere "technical problems."[3] Instead of hammering away at evolving challenges as if they were old problems, adaptive leaders understand the larger complexity of social change and the dynamics of innovation and learning needed right now. The Iron Age was upon the Israelites, and they were slow to catch up to the new technology of warfare. The loose tribal confederation was trying to figure out how to be a kingdom. If ever large-minded adaptive change was required, it was of King Saul; if ever someone was lacking in imagination and this sort of broad insight, it was King Saul.

Yet, even as we name his faults, we have to back up and confess that he was the one God wanted for that moment, superficially strong but inherently very weak—as if it suited God to put a weak one on the throne in order to drive the hidden plot of God's story. When we are rankled by poor leadership, could it be that there are larger forces at work than simply the weakness of the leader in question?

Much has been written about Saul as a tragic figure. The plot of his story is kin to those Greek dramas in which the main character (like Oedipus), no matter what he actually does, is fated into a destiny that simply cannot be altered. There are periods in history, or situations in the life of an organization, when some swirl of events seems to consume even the best leaders. When Saul became king, the nation was a fledgling thing, awkwardly new and not yet structured. And the neighboring armies were fierce and relentless. There are so many moments in time when leadership quite simply will fail, no matter who's leading or how.

But more important, the very fact that anybody became king was out of kilter and not in sync with God and Israel's best theological wisdom. David Gunn suggests that Saul is "vulnerable as an object-lesson," which the Lord wanted to teach a wayward people; he is "kingship's scapegoat" and "his future is loaded against him." "Saul walks a tightrope. He is caught in the midst of a situation of tension which is not of his own making and over which he has but limited control."[4] God made Saul king, but we sense even God had determined that he would fail. Samuel most assuredly hoped for his demise and hurried it along by nit picky fault-finding. Apart from large, historic forces that can be the ruin of leadership, there are always underminers with which to contend, and sometimes they win.

And yet if we ponder Greek tragedy, external circumstance isn't the only driver of the story's plot. Characters may also carry in themselves some hidden, tragic flaw, masked by their ability and achievement, that inexorably leads to downfall. Saul was passionate about God, but could we say he was too scrupulous? In 1 Samuel 13 and 15, we see him being anxious, and overly so, to perform his religious duties. The Bible's stories, in concert with much of civilization's finest literature, not to mention the annals of history, reveal how leadership is bedeviled by such seemingly minor but perilous flaws. In fact, all leaders have something—some sort of thorn in the side—and if this thorn is left unacknowledged, unnoticed, or unaddressed, it will cause much sorrow to the leader, those who follow, and even whole nations.

I had been in ministry nearly three decades when, finally, one of those anonymous "360" surveys enabled some of my coworkers to say that at times they find me cocky or unapproachable. The revelation of this particular flaw in me came as a shock. I would have counted myself as fragile in confidence but entirely approachable. My inner view of my flawedness, and their external view of my flawedness could not have been more different. And yet, we all saw the same, elusive thing. Awareness has helped, but these kinds of quirks are so deeply embedded they aren't easily fixed. Fortunately my flaw hasn't been fatal to the organization. Some unacknowledged flaws dole out a lot of pain and organizational dysfunction.

Inner Torments

Saul is thought to have suffered what today we would diagnose as mental illness. We witness his mounting anxiety, plunging him ever more deeply into paranoia and the resulting violent pursuit of David, which is unfortunate for Saul, as David had been the only one who could soothe Saul's inner torment. Early in our story, when a cloud descended over Saul, "David took the lyre and played it with his hand, and Saul would be relieved and feel better, and the evil spirit would depart from him" (1 Sam 16:23).

What, after all, is the relationship between leadership and mental illness? The psychiatrist Nassir Ghaemi has explored the way some of our most brilliant leaders—especially during times of crisis—have suffered from depression, mania, neuroticism, and other mood disorders.[5] We may be familiar with Churchill's "black dog," the intense darkness into which Lincoln would plunge, the overwhelming depression of Martin Luther King Jr., the near-suicidal bouts of agony endured by Gandhi, the scary symptoms exhibited by General William Sherman, or the frantic mania of media mogul Ted Turner—not to mention the self-evident insanity of tyrants like Adolf Hitler.

Ghaemi's best insight into the function of this suffering is downright biblical. It is not that these titans overcame their illness or managed to achieve much despite their illness. Ghaemi persuasively illustrates the way their mental distress was actually essential to their stellar leadership. Depression fosters sympathy for others. The ability to grasp the dark side of situations can lead to more realistic assessments. Survivors of inner torment develop a kind of resilience, without which leadership breaks down during times of duress. Sane, uncomplicated people (Neville Chamberlain and George W. Bush are Ghaemi's examples) do fine when all runs smoothly. But they simply do not have the right stuff during a crisis, never having suffered themselves. They are not weak enough to lead.

How many of the great saints, theologians, and heroes through Church history might Ghaemi analyze and discern to be laden with mental illness? Luther, surely; Francis, no doubt; Teresa of Avila, beyond question; and all those freakish ascetics like Simeon Stylites (squatting on a pillar for a few decades?). Can we imagine a search committee pleased that a prospective pastor suffers bouts of depression? Can we conceive of a day when a CEO's self-reported manic-depression would be cause for the people to think, *Now we are on the verge of stellar leadership?* Don't we hide our darkness? And at best seek ultraconfidential support if something is awry in our heads?

Eugene Rogers wrote that the Spirit has so arranged things that "our limitations are intended for our benefit."[6] Could it be that our darkness, our craziness, is not merely a burden to be overcome, but might be an actual gift of the Spirit to the church and other institutions? And not merely to those individuals among the body who battle darkness but actually the church as the endangered institution that it is? If the church is indeed in its own "dark night,"[7] don't we need the unstable—those who have barely hung on by a thread—women and men who, having been to the abyss, are weak enough to lead in the dark?

Study Questions

1. Why do nations, cities, and churches so often want the wrong kind of leaders?

2. How do you feel about this notion that God "gives us up" to our sinful wishes—but then actually redeems it all?

3. When have you seen larger historical forces define a given leader's failure or success?

4. When have you seen underminers subverting leadership?

5. How often does sheer luck come into play for leaders and organizations?

6. What is your tragic flaw? What tragic flaws have you seen in others?

7. In our society, which averts its gaze from mental illness, do you believe a leader might lead well, or poorly, because of inner struggles?

DAVID

The Natural

From the very beginning, poor Saul was pretty much done. He would cling to power for a while, and yet any authority his kingship might have had was over. But kingship itself was only getting started, and it continued with considerable flair, havoc, and drama with David. When Saul first walked onto the stage, he was big, very big. When David first appeared, he was small.

Already we see the Bible's quirky logic in play. "Not by might, nor by power, but by my Spirit, says the LORD of hosts" (Zech 4:6). "There is a boy here who has five barley loaves and two fish. But what are they among so many people?" (John 6:9). "It was not because you were more numerous than any other people that the LORD set his heart on you...for you were the fewest of all peoples" (Deut 7:7). "God chose what is foolish in the world to shame the wise; God chose what is weak in the world to shame the strong; God chose what is low and despised" (1 Cor 1:27-28).

David was small. Later on, he proved himself to be quite strong and clever—to a fault. In a theologically profound scene that says much about biblical leadership, Samuel made a clandestine visit to Bethlehem to anoint a new king, or perhaps we should say a king-in-waiting, since Saul was however shakily still on the throne. What were Jesse's feelings when he learned one of his sons would be king? Pride? Shock? A fearful trembling? He called them together and lined them up by age, height, and brawn. But one-by-one, Samuel dismissed them: the strapping Eliab, the burly Abinadab, the finely chiseled Shammah. Seven altogether.

The Lord spoke each time to Samuel—but how? Did the others hear? Was it a whisper? An interior voice? The Lord said, "Do not look on his appearance or on the height of his stature, because I have rejected him; for the LORD does not see as mortals see; they look on the outward appearance, but the LORD looks on the heart" (1 Sam 16:7). If we are to speak meaningfully of biblical leadership, this is the place to start: it isn't about ability, strength, IQ, street smarts, agility, or savvy. It's about the "heart"—although really it's just about God choosing whom God chooses.

Puzzled, Samuel shrugged. Only then did Jesse acknowledge that, well, yes, "There remains yet the youngest, but he is keeping the sheep" (v. 11). The obvious deduction is that Jesse didn't even consider the possibility that this little one might be the one. But could it be that Jesse actually feared David might be the one, that he saw unprecedented potential in him? Or perhaps he was simply the one he loved the most—the unexpected child of old age, the apple of his eye? The writer does take note that David "was ruddy, and had beautiful eyes, and was handsome" (v. 12). Perhaps Jesse wanted to keep this small but handsome one home to shelter him for himself and from the perils of kingship.

Christian history features so many stories of parents blocking their children's calling to sainthood. Francis of Assisi's father, Pietro, was so mortified when his son began giving to the poor with total abandon that he took him to court and disowned him. Pope Francis's mother was crushed when he reported he was headed into the priesthood instead of to medical school, and she would not speak to him or forgive him for some time. How many women and men never became great heroes of the church because parents restrained them and wouldn't let go?

Seeing Underground Things

Francesca Alan Murphy points out that there is not one divine miracle in the entire sixteen chapters of the story of David's rise from obscurity to power. As she puts it, "God's working has gone underground."[1] Leaders understand that God's working generally *is* underground; rarely does anything remotely miraculous save the day. What matters is trusting that God's working is still going on, as unseen as water being soaked up by the roots of a tree.

Or maybe we develop a different kind of seeing. The verb *see* (*ra'ah*) occurs six times in the story of David's anointing; "the LORD does not see as mortals see" (v. 7). How does God see? How can we see as God sees? Can we see things as they really are instead of being deceived by what is only superficially visible? As Gandalf wrote in a letter to Frodo in *The Lord of the Rings*, "All that is gold does not glitter."[2] Or that Native American saying: "We teach our children to see when there is nothing to see, and to listen where there is nothing to hear." It's a commonplace to say a leader is responsible for having a vision; 1 Samuel's take might be that the leader is someone who can see and who sees clearly and deeply.

The Hebrew word for "see," *ra'ah*, is one barely distinguishable sound away from *ra'ah*, the word for "shepherd." We might think of shepherds as lowly and despised, poor laborers of no account. Yet there is always an ambiguity to the image of a shepherd. Yes, they spent their days and nights out of doors with smelly animals who tended to nibble themselves lost. Mothers didn't fantasize that their daughters would marry shepherds one day. And yet in the agrarian, pastoral culture of the world in those days, where sheep were everywhere and they mattered for survival, even the mightiest kings of Sumer, Babylon, Assyria, and Egypt were often dubbed the "shepherds" of their people. David was a shepherd boy, but his responsibilities—to care for the flock, ensure they got food and water, protect them from harm, bring them safely home— were identical to those of the good ruler.

The absence of God's direct action in this story, especially as we turn the page from 1 Samuel to 2 Samuel, raises so many questions. Gerhard von Rad rather eloquently suggested the following:

> The author depicts a succession of occurrences in which the chain of inherent cause and effect is firmly knit up—so firmly indeed that the human eye discerns no point at which God could have put in his hand.

Yet secretly it is he who has brought all to pass; all the threads are in his hands.³

Don't many of our stories wind up like David's? Public events and private lives twist, turn, and collide. The pursuit of power and pleasure gets mixed up with efforts to be pious and faithful, and the results are mixed: some success and some disaster. Today's leaders humbly realize what Bible leaders experienced: they do their best, but then the cruel processes of history steamroll everybody—yet somehow they almost accidentally further God's kingdom. Does God cause or even superintend all this? Human leadership, in the church and in the world, has to live with this mystery: where is God in it all? There are hints, clues, guesses, wonderings. But who can be sure?

Who Is God and Who Isn't

Consider the thrilling episode you may have adored as a child (although as an adult you shudder when you realize its climax is grisly): the battle between David and Goliath. The battle has a fairy-tale feel to it, but if we're attentive, there's a lot there. Why does it resonate even with grown people? Francesca Murphy may be right: "It is because we yearn to believe that 'strength is made perfect in weakness' (2 Cor 12:9 [KJV])."⁴ David was still small. His role in the war with the Philistines was to carry his big brother's lunchboxes. But this small one was the one who rose to Goliath's challenge.

King Saul, tall and covered with armor, was the official leader. And yet David was the one who led. The Bible's crazed logic comes into play: "A little child shall lead them" (Isa 11:6). It was the little one, the laughable one, the one who felt clumsy in the armor no soldier would do without, who won the day. Unprotected, unknown, uncredentialed, David was small enough, even weak enough, to lead.

We wouldn't extract "leadership principles" from this story, or we'd be putting little kids with pluck in charge of all the big churches and companies. Malcolm Gladwell wrote about cases where the underdog wins through cunning and surprise and how a disadvantage can become an advantage; he titled his book *David and Goliath.*[5]

Our story in 1 Samuel 17 is very different. It's not that the underdog beat the big guy. The real confrontation that day was theological. The question was not *Who can beat the other guy?* but rather *Who is God and Who isn't?* David brazenly responded to Goliath's mockery by saying,

> You come to me with sword and spear and javelin; but I come to you in the name of the LORD of hosts...whom you have defied. This very day the LORD will deliver you into my hand...so that all the earth may know that there is a God in Israel, and that all this assembly may know that the LORD does not save by sword and spear. (1 Sam 17:45-47)

Goliath had a hilariously unfair advantage in size and armor, but he did not have "the whole armor of God" (Eph 6:11). Who is God? Not Goliath or the Philistine deity, and not even David, the small one.

There are moments when the leadership required is for somebody, anybody really, to stand up for God, to insist on what is right—even if everyone else chuckles, even if the one standing up is unarmed and doesn't stand a chance. Many times in my ministry such crucial moments have presented themselves. Sometimes I've taken my stand. Sometimes I've leaned forward but too carefully. Sometimes I've slinked away to safety. Sometimes I've failed to notice that *now* is the crucial moment. And sometimes I've thought I was defending God's honor when really I was picking a fight for myself. Courage, discernment, and humility are what we need and pray for.

Saul had been on point when he pushed back: "You are not able to go against this Philistine" (1 Sam 17:33). David listed a few of his achievements, but Saul was right: David was not able. It is not human ability that will finally achieve God's good end and deliver God's people. Yes, David whirled his slingshot and planted the first stone into the lone unarmored spot on Goliath's huge body, right between the eyes. Was this a divinely directed shot? Incredible skill? Luck? All three? When God's work gets done, when good unfolds, is it skill, providence, chance, or some holy and secular mix of them all?

David does appear to be something of what Peter Drucker would call a "natural,"[6] someone with confidence who effortlessly inspires and understands priorities. David's shedding of conventional weaponry is intriguing, isn't it? Do we stick with tried and true methods? With what has always been effective? When can leaders travel a little lighter, experimenting with the unconventional? Can we get out of a rut by asking a real child? Or at least asking what impact our action might have on a small child? I know a real estate developer who got involved in educational equity in his spare time. Realizing one of his projects would unwittingly contribute to skewed disadvantages for children not far from his project, he altered his plan, made allowances for poorer residents, didn't cash in as much profit as he could have, but did what he believed God was asking him to do.

Authority and Grand Gestures

The rest of the story of David's rise to power, and then his struggles and eventual decline, is high drama. All kinds of leadership quandaries are on display in several episodes in his life. Celebrating David's successes in battle, the people chant, "Saul has killed his thousands, / and David his ten thousands" (1 Sam 18:7). Saul might have beamed with pride over his prodigy. But envy got the upper hand and soured their relationship. How often does sheer jealousy impact the dynamics of a business, a church, a family? What imbalance in the soul prods us to resent the success of someone else or even to relish another's failure? Exploring Saul's jealousy, Lewis Parks and Bruce Birch ask, "Why is it so hard for leaders to bless the lives they have been given rather than curse the ones they haven't?"[7]

A pair of dramatic encounters show us David at his noblest. Three thousand crack troops followed Saul all the way south to En-gedi (1 Sam 24). Saul, quite naturally but in a less-than-regal manner, went in to a cave to relieve himself. David, by sheer luck, was hiding in that very cave. When David's men realized the opportunity David had been given to put an end to Saul's murderous pursuit, they had to cover their mouths lest they burst out in glee. But David let his chance for power slide on by. He furtively cut off the corner of Saul's cloak—and then felt guilty about it!

Not long after this, David managed to find his way into Saul's camp one night and found Saul sound asleep with his spear propped right next to his head. Despite Abishai's urging, David again let Saul, his avowed enemy, live. He did keep the spear, so Saul would know.

This leader did not seize the reins of leadership. Instead of assuming power, which he could have done easily (and who would have blamed him?), he let the institution be what it was and kept to his place in it. He let time take its course; as Walter Brueggemann put it, 1 Samuel "reports the slow, steady working out of God's purpose. David need not hurry that process, even as he need not doubt it."[8] Beyond any question, by behaving so honorably, his authority soared even though he still had no official power. Leadership is about authority far more than power. There is some virtue to restraint, and to mercy, and the real leader often is the one who is the humblest and does not step to the fore when the opening presents itself.

These two vignettes remind us that institutions need what Lovett Weems calls "grand gestures."[9] David didn't kill Saul, but he didn't do nothing. He made the point that he was for peace, that he didn't want to kill his enemy even when he could have. Jesus, after all, told us to love our enemies just as he loved his. But how? The possibility of a dramatic gesture might present itself.

Francis of Assisi traveled with an army of Crusaders to fight the dreaded Muslims. With the two bloodthirsty (and frankly, terrified) armies arrayed on either side of no-man's-land, Francis, unarmed, simply walked to the Muslim side. They drew their sabers, but he was so pitiful they didn't kill him and instead took him to the sultan, Malik al-Kamil. They became friends, and peace was won, if only for a short time. Rosa Parks refused to get up from her seat on a bus in Montgomery, Alabama.

A few weeks later, the aged Mother Pollard refused a ride to work, saying, "My feets is tired, but my soul is rested." Pope Francis, hoping his belief in mercy might catch on and spread like a contagion, offered a chair to the Swiss guard outside his office; embraced Vinicio Riva, a man suffering from neurofibromatosis and a lifetime of social ridicule; and washed the feet of incarcerated Muslims, including a woman.

Danny Meyer believes his restaurants are extraordinarily successful because his people intentionally exceed expectations. "I encourage each manager to take ten minutes a day to make three gestures that exceed expectations and take a special interest in our guests. That translates to 1,000 such gestures every year."[10]

Even if you aren't in a restaurant, a grand gesture might be as simple as a telephone call, showing up unexpectedly, or being gracious when the opposite is expected.

Peter Drucker has shown how the most effective business managers inspire loyalty throughout the ranks. But you can't just claim loyalty or buy it.

> One must be worthy of it. To be so, managers must set high standards and live by example.... Those leaders who inspire loyalty raise the morale of their people, which in turn enhances performance. Remember that loyalty is a two-way street. Managers must practice what they preach by being loyal to their employees.[11]

Who wouldn't be doggedly loyal to David? Consider the time David was hemmed in by the Philistines and, without asking for a thing, simply said, "O that someone would give me water to drink from the well of Bethlehem" (2 Sam 23:15). Perhaps as impulsively as the four knights who heard Henry II's complaint about Thomas Becket and promptly rode to Canterbury and killed him, three of David's warriors

> broke through the camp of the Philistines, drew water from the well of Bethlehem that was by the gate, and brought it to David. But he would not drink of it; he poured it out to the LORD, for he said "The LORD forbid that I should do this. Can I drink the blood of the men who went at the risk of their lives?" (vv. 16-17)

His poignant refusal to drink earned him more loyalty than a thousand personal favors. What gestures of refusal enable leaders to lead?

Similarly, David refused to dispose of the lone survivor from Saul's family. Mephibosheth was "crippled in his feet," a condition made worse when he was dropped by his nurse (4:4). David mercifully provided him with property and caregivers. Jean Vanier has taught us much about the way those who have disabilities can actually lead the rest of us, humanizing us, reminding us of the simplicity of joy and love.

> We are afraid of showing weakness. We are afraid of not succeeding. Deep inside we are afraid of not being recognized. So we pretend we are the best. We hide behind power. We hide behind all sorts of things. However, when we meet people with disabilities and reveal to them through our eyes and ears words that they are precious, they are changed. But we too are changed. We are led to God.[12]

Often, someone facing unusual challenges appears in our circle. The faithful leader is weak enough to treat this seemingly weak one graciously, understanding the broader impact that tender care for just one person can be a blessing to everyone.

Finally, after a hopeless battle at Mount Gilboa, Saul died. David grieved, and we needn't think he was faking it for public consumption. The author of 1 and 2 Samuel plainly believed God wanted David, and not Saul, to be king—but why? David was hardly holier than Saul. Perhaps God had a lesson to teach the people. They had asked for a king; God let them have what they asked for, and it was not pretty. With David, God begins to use their foolish request for God's higher purpose.

First Among Equals

Something else inherent in biblical leadership is hidden away in 2 Samuel 5, which tells us of the day at Hebron when David was acclaimed as Saul's successor. Readers of English might miss the subtle but theologically profound nuances to the story. The tribes gathered and spoke of the days when Saul became "king" (*melek*). But then, turning to David, they added, "The LORD said to you: It is you who…shall be ruler" (*nāgîd*, not *melek*). All other nations (and the people's trouble began when they wanted to be like the other nations!) spoke of their king as *melek*. But the Lord called David not *melek* but *nāgîd*, which implies something more like "prince," maybe even the crown prince.

What a theologically useful distinction this was! The Lord alone is king (*melek*), but Israel now had a ruler (*nāgîd*)—a "crown prince" to the Lord if you will. At the pinnacle of human authority in Israel stood someone who was a dependent subject to the true king. The king had no absolute power but was just as answerable to God's law as everyone else. The Bible reminds us that a leader is not a superior being and has no significant status others don't. At their best, leaders can be like those consuls in the Roman Republic who were not dictators but simply role-fillers, each one nothing more than a *primus inter pares*, "first among equals," and only for a time and only in a particular role.

What is ministerial leadership about? The ordained woman has no special status; the ordained man isn't on some higher plane. What the ordained person does is entirely "representative" in nature.[13] When the clergy visit and pray in the hospital, it is as the representative of the entire Body of Christ; when the clergy preach or preside, it is as one of the family called to this particular task that matters for the Body. Corporate and community leadership could benefit from this same sort of vision.

Who was Jesus after all? Jesus was divine, God in the flesh. But the Gospels are at pains to persuade us that Jesus really was one of us; he wasn't play-acting. He subjected himself to God the Father's kingship. Jesus's leadership, when it was at its most compelling, was when Jesus was hungry, thirsty, praying in agony, and even dying and being hauled away into a tomb. Jesus became king when he stood in silence before Pilate's question about his kingship, when he yielded everything to the King of kings, the God who seemed to have forsaken Jesus in death in the same way we all feel forsaken. Biblical leadership looks a lot like the Garden of Gethsemane, Golgotha, and therefore, thankfully, the empty tomb.

Leadership Betrayed in Private Moments

Patrick Lencioni is surely right when he explains that "the single greatest advantage any company can achieve is organizational health."[14] It would be hard to imagine an organization more unhealthy and down-right dysfunctional than David's. His family, so integral to a monarchy, was the stuff of soap opera. His relationships with his officials were tense with poor communication, power plays, and fractured priorities. Lencioni speaks of the "five dysfunctions of a team."[15] David's team had a dozen or more.

David's problems, and all the subsequent disasters for his family and the whole nation, came when he strayed, like a lost sheep, from this accountability to God's law when he behaved like the kings of the other nations. Most notoriously, he saw a beautiful woman and then seized her in what we could only characterize as unbridled lust. Lust isn't mere sexual desire; lust is treating another person as less than a person, as an object for one's own gratification. The writer of 2 Samuel 11:3 underlines that she was not a plaything: she was someone's daughter (Eliam's) and someone's wife (Uriah's).

David illustrates what we know all too painfully: leadership is squandered more often in private moments than in public acts. Strength perverted, and weakness unacknowledged, opens up an intricate web of crazed confusion and hurt. Bathsheba was only the first victim. Uriah and other innocent soldiers died. David's sons Amnon, Absalom, and Adonijah took after their father by misbehaving sexually and following up with violence. A civil war erupted. More people were killed, wives were widowed, and children were orphaned. The nation fell apart.

This is the degeneracy of leadership. One seemingly small lapse sets off the dominoes, and the pain rifles through institutions and families. Even if the cover-up is successful the dysfunction of self never segregates itself well enough. If you can be creepy in private, that lack of integrity creeps unnoticed into every arena. Something is wrong, and no one quite knows what it might be.

Of course, God knows. David might have deluded himself into thinking God didn't know, but God sent Nathan to confront the king. Israel did not yet have prophets, but Nathan was their forefather. He told hard truth to corrupt power. As Tim Laniak put it, Nathan exposed "just how far David had come from being the shepherd of God's people: rather than protecting them on the battlefield, he was at home sacrificing them for his personal pleasure."[16] And Nathan did so quite shrewdly by spinning a clever story that lured David in to the realization of the dastardly motives and harrowing scope of the cluster of his evil deeds.

David's relationships with various women were complicated, usually unseemly, yet often quite lucky for him. David Wolpe went so far as to suggest that "it seems that when David needs a miracle, God finds a woman to enact it in a worldly manner."[17] Certainly his career received several boosts because of the women he married. Consider Abigail. David demonstrated peculiar leadership savvy by hatching a scheme to protect her husband Nabal's sheep (1 Sam 24)—although Nabal only learned about it when David and his men (with drawn swords) asked him to pay up. As Wolpe humorously put it, "Without the benefit of the *Godfather* movies," Nabal did not understand "an offer you cannot refuse."[18] Abigail intervened. Nabal got drunk and fell asleep. On waking up, and realizing how much his wife loathed him, Nabal had a heart attack and died. Without lifting a finger, David got rid of an enemy and gained a wife and her wealth. Jim Collins memorably spoke of leadership as getting the right people on the bus and the wrong people off;[19] David most ruthlessly shed those who weren't with his program.

Complications of Marriage and Parenting

In what surely was David's crudest manipulation of a woman, he married Saul's daughter Michal, and then he was done with her except to treat her with contempt. She despised his provocative dance when the ark arrived in Jerusalem. Robert Barron wondered: What is to be made of Michal's aversion to David's dancing as she gazed down through her window?

> One can only begin to imagine the texture of her feelings at this point in the narrative. She had witnessed the deaths of her father and brother and the fall of Saul's kingdom; her husband had gone on to marry several other women and fathered children with them while she remained childless.... From her height, she regards David with the same haughty disdain that her father once showed to his rival.[20]

Of course, she was resentful, angry, even humiliated.

David's minimal clothing had a clear sexual connotation, foreshadowing future disasters resulting from his sexual imprudence and how his romantic relationships determined his leadership. Bathsheba, whom he stuck with even after their lovechild was born and died, became a master manipulator of things political from her secure place in the palace. Some have suggested that David never really loved. He was loved, indeed. But for his part, he seems to fall in that category of do-anything people who know how to get ahead and see people, even spouses and children, as pawns in a high-risk game of power.

David illustrates in dramatic fashion the peculiar role family plays, not just in a leader's life but in his very leading. How little do we grasp the dynamics of family in leadership situations? Peter Scazzero's "emotionally healthy leadership" model requires you to explore your genogram to understand how your family of origin is always perched on your shoulder wherever you do any kind of leading, and their craziness rattles in you and then spreads outward to everybody else.[21]

David's relationships with his children were all complex and eventually hurtful. He loved them dearly, probably excessively. He could not be firm with them. This indulgence left them plenty of room to maneuver, scheme, and even kill one another, all breaking his heart. David Wolpe asks, "Did David reflect on the parallels between his own conduct and that of his children?"[22] If so, he must have shuddered and sunk into the deepest of funks. Joab, David's nephew and commander of his army, chided David for his overwrought grief after the death of Absalom, who was fomenting a revolution and would have taken David's life in a heartbeat! But David could not help himself; he could not rule as shrewdly as he might because his knees were buckled by the sorrows of family.

Yet as we ponder David's agonizing life with his grown children, we may pause and be profoundly moved by Robert Barron's question: "Does David's 'weakness' for his children, his sentimental failure to exact true justice in their regard, in fact not represent the deeper and higher judgment of God?"[23] Indeed. David loved his children, like Absalom, even in rebellion against him. And when Absalom died, David grieved heavily over the loss of this wayward son. God's love is like this: loving relentlessly even those in staunch rebellion against God. Sometimes we see what appears to be an abdication of strong leadership, an excess of indulgent kindness—but could this very failure to lead well serve as a witness to God's unfailing patience and mercy toward us?

Kings as Spiritual Leaders

Mothers don't want their sons to grow up to be like King David. He's dangerous to be around. He's a mess internally. He'll break your heart. Adjectives like *machiavellian, calculating,* and *prodigal* come to mind. And yet throughout the story his piety not only manifests itself but it seems in some curious way to define him. Clearly he was a boy and then a man with a keen sense of God's presence, help, and even judgment. His faith was entirely genuine, despite his flaws—or perhaps because of them.

Walking onto the stage at the opening of Israel's history as a nation, David and those around him were trying to figure out how things should be. As king, he had responsibility not only for Israel's political life but also its spiritual life. He fulfilled functions we usually associate with a priest. He offered sacrifice. He brought the ark into his new capital city of Jerusalem and led the people in enthusiastic worship in a manner that struck his wife Michal and surely many others as over the top (2 Sam 6). Was he tantalizingly over-exuberant? Or genuinely worshipful?

If we had seen him, would we have shuddered, as Michal did? Or would we see his giddy dance as a distant echo of Jesus and his adoring crowds when he entered that same city on Palm Sunday?

He was not the only king who functioned like a priest. Solomon sacrificed at Gibeon (1 Kgs 3:4) and led the ceremony dedicating the temple (1 Kgs 8). The initiative for religious reformation, which we expect from outsiders to power, like Martin Luther or St. Francis, was assumed by kings: Jehoshaphat (1 Kgs 22) and Hezekiah (2 Kgs 18) rid Israel of idolatrous worship. Josiah (2 Kgs 23) more dramatically took on the task of restoring the temple facilities, which had fallen into disrepair. During renovations, a scroll was discovered—some long-ignored scriptures. King Josiah read God's word, wept, repented, and demanded radical change across the entire country's religious practice.

Of course, other kings were virtual antireformers, creating the very need for the reform. Solomon, not nearly as wise as he was reported to be, built temples to foreign gods to placate his foreign wives and thereby made a sham of the holy city's dedication to the one true God (1 Kgs 11:7). Ahab built a temple to Baal to placate his conniving wife, Jezebel (1 Kgs 16:32).

In Israel, the king was expected to be a spiritual leader. There was no separation of religion and state. Today, leaders of all kinds, not just in church life but also in business and politics, wield immense spiritual influence that is rarely acknowledged. The tone they set by their priorities, and the mood they create among citizens, has profound and lasting effects on what people think about God and what is ultimately worthwhile. A powerful business leader thinks he's merely turning profits for shareholders, but the impact on the values and lives of people he'll never meet can be insidious. A popular politician can stir people up into a frenzy by her vision that may not be remotely in sync with God's. Perhaps rarely, but yet most definitely, a holy, humble leader in business and politics can change the outlook and sense of God among the masses.

Study Questions

1. What does it mean "to see as the Lord sees"?

2. Do you believe Jesse didn't think David was the one? Or that he knew he probably was the one?

3. How do parental expectations confuse or get mixed up with what God calls someone to be or do?

4. When God seems absent from your life, or the life of the world, is God working underground? And if so, how?

5. Can you think of an example of an "extraordinary gesture" and how the authority won by it?

6. When have you seen people with weakness, with disabilities, have a helpful impact on others?

7. Why is it that leadership is squandered more often in private moments than in public acts? And is this so, even if the private misdeeds aren't found out?

8. Home life matters in leadership. How can we best deal with the complications of marital and parenting challenges in ourselves and others?

9. Do our political leaders have an inevitable impact on the spiritual lives of all of us? And if so, how?

KINGS AND A QUEEN

Failures and Providence

We can glide quickly over the annals of the rest of the kings, for there is a monotony, a repetitiveness about their failures, punctuated by an occasional spasm of fidelity then a quick return to the long, dull saga of kings trying pathetically to be kings "like the nations." Solomon is the extreme example of what unfolds. He is a larger-than-life figure, and it's hard to get any feel for what he might have been like inside his own skin—a dramatic contrast to his father, David, whose moods and passions are splayed over every page of our story.

Solomon was extraordinarily gifted. His wisdom was legendary. And who ever prayed more humbly and in a theologically profound way than young Solomon early in his career?

> O Lord my God, you have made your servant king in place of my father David, although I am only a little child; I do not know how to go out or come in.... Give your servant therefore an understanding mind to govern your people, able to discern between good and evil; for who can govern this your great people? (1 Kgs 3:7, 9)

He didn't ask for success, might, or glory but simply wisdom, with a humble yielding to God.

The Problem with Success

And yet success, might, and glory are precisely what flowed into Solomon's kingdom. The childlike humility of his prayer didn't stick. Had what we know as the "prosperity gospel" existed in the early Iron Age, Solomon would have been its poster boy. Dizzyingly successful, the epitome of strength: his buildings dazzled, his regiments impressed, his wealth mounted. Surely God was blessing him and the nation. The temple he constructed left the masses in awe of his piety, although there is little doubt that Solomon was the kind of leader who fancied the notion of capturing God in a box, retrievable when needed.

Then there were the women. In the stories about Solomon in 1 Kings, we get no glimpse of anything romantic—not a single illicit rendezvous, no real relationships at all. With hundreds of wives and concubines, how could feelings enter in? First Kings reports that Solomon made shrewd political pacts that involved marriages to the daughters of foreign potentates, which sealed trade advantages and military protection. This was what all brilliant rulers did in those days.

But to accommodate them, in a way that seems entirely charitable and open-minded in our culture, Solomon built sanctuaries for the worship of their native gods from back home in Egypt, Sidon, and Moab. What an enlightened despot; what a gracious husband! And yet his sworn responsibility was to inspire fidelity to the only true God. The religious confusion he introduced sowed the seeds for centuries of idolatry to come.

Already in Solomon's time, we can see what mixing worship of the biblical God with other gods inevitably ushered into society: forced labor, slavery, and the severe oppression of the people of Israel—exactly what Samuel had ominously warned the people would happen (1 Sam 8). Leaders who strive to be Christian are to be vigilant about the insidious, downright sneaky ways socioeconomic agendas seep in and damage the real people being led. Solomon's theological failure was an invitation to worldly ways of organizing human life that were not of God and not beneficial to people.

43

We need not be surprised. He had come to power through plotting and subterfuge. The sordid actions of David's sons, wives, and generals jockeying for position guaranteed that the result would not be holy. How leadership comes to be and how leadership commences fashions the framework within which leadership will honor God or poison the well.

Despite all the massive stone structures that made Solomon's city appear to be impregnable, the theological and political foundations were flimsy. We are reminded of King Herod's world-renowned building program with the temple in Jerusalem as its crown jewel. The authorities put Jesus to death because of his dire warning, which did in fact come true, that "not one stone will be left here upon another" (Mark 13:2). Within minutes of Solomon's death, his masterfully constructed kingdom fell apart.

The people convened around the new king, Solomon's son Rehoboam. They asked for some relief: "Your father made our yoke heavy. Now therefore lighten the hard service of your father and his heavy yoke...and we will serve you" (1 Kgs 12:4). He responded by saying he needed three days to think about it. The older sages wisely counseled him: "If you will be a servant to this people...and speak good words to them when you answer them, then they will be your servants forever" (v. 7). How lovely, this path toward servant leadership. Rehoboam had this narrow window to turn things around.

"But" [such an ominous word] "he disregarded the advice that the older men gave him, and consulted with the young men who had grown up with him and now attended him" (v. 8). Leadership's most important question is this: With whom will you surround yourself? To whom do you listen? These cocky young pups appealed to the testosterone in him with their tough talk: "Thus you should say to them, 'My little finger is thicker than my father's loins.... Whereas my father laid on you a heavy yoke, I will add to your yoke. My father disciplined you with whips, but I will discipline you with scorpions'" (vv. 10-11). Somehow, these words sounded right to this sophomoric juvenile. We can picture him snarling, chest sticking out, and the trembling horror among the people.

With one brief speech he squandered his kingdom. He was way too strong to lead. How fragile is emotional capital? How tenuous is trust in leadership?

Rehoboam might strike us as absurd. But his is a cautionary tale, for Jean Vanier is right: "Inside each of us is a little tyrant who wants power and the associated prestige, who wants to dominate, to be superior and to control."[1] Strong leaders are rarely cognizant of the demons perched on their shoulders feeding that little tyrant. Simply asking the question *Are you weak enough to lead?* can be a healthy, humbling corrective, helping to hold the tyrant at bay.

Not surprisingly, a vast segment of Rehoboam's kingdom broke away. The leadership of the breakaway group was no better. The seceding tribes pieced together a government and established a capital in the north. Their new king, Jeroboam, knew they needed God—and he knew their craving to be "like the nations" and their susceptibility to the shiny gods of those nations. So he fashioned golden calves, which must have drawn raucous cheers from crowds. But God's heart was grieved, and the people were unwittingly being misled. Good leadership isn't about popularity or merely giving people what they want.

God's Subversive Way

Solomon, Rehoboam, and Jeroboam kicked off a long chronicle of one king after another, the vast majority grasping for power, mimicking the other nations, failing the Lord and their people time after time. Curiously, the other nations evaluated these kings very differently. Consider Omri and his son Ahab. If all we knew about Omri's dynasty came from the envying remarks of Israel's powerful neighbors, we could count them as the greatest of all of Israel's rulers. They flexed their political, economic, and military muscle in such prodigious ways that even the vaunted Assyrians were impressed.

But in Israel, they were assessed as failures, nasty perils, the real low point of Israel's history. Omri and Ahab were "effective," but they had no respect for Israel's sacred traditions; faith in the true God, holy living, and faithful governing took a back seat. These kings were so strong they became enemies of holiness and justice.

In the face of the success the world adores, there is such a thing as divine judgment. The Christian leader's tough decision is whether to be like Omri and press for the max or to rest easy with far less success. Consider King Hezekiah. The Assyrians mocked his weakness. During the siege of Jerusalem, the mighty Sennacherib boasted that Hezekiah was shut up "like a bird in a cage." But weak Hezekiah was praised by 1 Kings for his faithfulness and holy submission to God's will. We might wish not to have to make such a choice; much discernment and courage are required. We are reminded of Paul's words: "Has not God made foolish the wisdom of the world? . . . God's weakness is stronger than human strength" (1 Cor 1:20, 25).

If we can imagine God engaging in an annual performance review of the king, we would see that God had lofty expectations—or perhaps we should say "lowly" expectations. God's vision for the king wasn't about anything high and mighty. The duty of the king, outlined with clarity in the liturgy used at his coronation, was to go low, be with the lowly, and lift them up.

> Give the king your justice, O God.
> . . . .
> May he judge your people with righteousness,
> and your poor with justice.
> . . . .
> May he defend the cause of the poor of the people,
> give deliverance to the needy
> . . . .
> In his days may righteousness flourish
> and peace abound
> . . . .
> For he delivers the needy when they call,
> the poor and those who have no helper.

He has pity on the weak and the needy

. . . .

May prayer be made for him continually (Ps 72:1, 2, 4, 7, 12, 13, 15)

We should be flabbergasted and frankly full of trepidation when we read this, God's holy will for the king, for this is a far cry from what we demand of our leaders. We vote for the one who will make me richer, who will defend my interests. But the Israelite king's first and central task was to bring justice, aid, and care for the poor, for those who have no advocate. The measure of the king's reign was whether there was righteousness or not; we look to gauges like the stock market. The psalm asks that prayer be made for the king continually. What if we invested as much time and passion in prayer for the president as we do in grousing about him or second-guessing policy? What if our corporate evaluation tools began with questions about goodness and community engagement instead of treating them as extra credit?

God raised these questions and provided unwanted evaluations to these strong rulers by way of the prophets. First Nathan, then Elijah, Elisha, Micaiah, and the rest inserted themselves into the frightfully dull saga of one king after another botching things. Their interactions with the powers that be are unfailingly fascinating as we will see in our next chapter when we turn to a very different sort of leadership: the prophets of Israel.

Esther, Luck and Providence

Before we do, let's ponder a rarity in scripture: a story about a queen. And not an Israelite queen, but a Persian! How this Israelite woman became a Persian queen, and what she then pulled off, is high drama. Wielding absolutely no official political power, Esther changed the course of history for Israel, and even Persia. She may fit what leadership guru Ron Heifetz called "leadership without authority"[2]—something entirely familiar to women through history. This riveting story recounts a season when the Persian King Xerxes I (called Ahasuerus in the Bible) was dissed by his wife, Queen Vashti, which provoked him into conducting a beauty pageant to replace her. Esther won—in the nick of time, too, as the wicked Haman was plotting the extermination of the Jews.

Heifetz notices the way unauthorized leaders sometimes straddle boundaries to create a new perspective. In Esther's case, she was the Persian queen but still a Jew, and she hatched a plan to have both the unwitting king and the evil-plotting Haman at dinner together so she could expose Haman's plan—deploying what Heifetz would call "creative deviance."[3]

What is even more intriguing for the would-be Christian leader is the rather shocking fact that the Hebrew text of the book of Esther never mentions God. But was God absent? Mordecai, Esther's older cousin, by "chance" stumbled upon information about Haman's plans. Xerxes, by "chance," couldn't sleep one night; to pass the hours, he thumbed through the royal archives and happened upon a mention of Mordecai's heroism. Was all this sheer luck? There really is such a thing as luck, good and bad, and leaders have to deal with plenty of it.

But in Esther's story, as in David's rise to power, aren't we invited to see that the hand of God in some mysterious way is orchestrating things? There are holes in the story where we expect God to have acted. As David Clines put it, those holes are "God-shaped. To the religious believer, 'chance' is a name for God."[4] Maybe so. But Esther still had to act, and with considerable pluck, as Clines acknowledges: "Without the protagonists' courage and craft the coincidences would have fallen to the ground; and without the coincidences, all the wit in the world would not have saved the Jewish people."[5]

Study Questions

1. Why is it a problem when gifted leaders like Solomon actually achieve so much?

2. What are some sneaky ways unholy agendas find their way into business and political leadership?

3. When have you heard good counsel, or foolish counsel? And how did you respond?

4. Can you think of leadership that has been godly but ineffective in the world's eyes? Or effective but ungodly?

5. How do we discern the interplay of luck, chance, courageous action, and divine providence?

ELIJAH

Loneliness and Renewal

I n our last chapter, we reviewed how, as decade after decade unfolded, one king after another tried to be "like the nations," with predictable, sorry results. The story is boring and depressing. During those centuries, the most dramatic and interesting moments in Israel's history were when prophets spoke up. Once in a while, somebody asked, "Is there any word from the Lord?" and sought out a prophet. Most of the time, the prophet simply intruded, unwelcome and often disliked. Kings chafed under their words, or sneered or retaliated.

With the prophets we see a different kind of leadership. They held no office. Whatever authority they had was noninstitutional. They spoke from outside the system, delivering a word of critique when kings and people were unholy or just plain lost, and then also a word of hope when the institution was in ruins and the people were forlorn. The daunting challenge today is how to be a prophetic leader when you find yourself inside or even in charge of the very institution in need of that external prophetic word. A tougher challenge can be to welcome a prophetic word when it comes and not get defensive. As Ron Heifetz and Donald Laurie remind us, leaders need to "protect leadership voices from below,"[1] the whistleblowers, whiners, critics, and creative deviants who ask awkward questions or sow discontent.

We know fifty-five prophets by name, fifteen of whom have biblical books named for them. But there were hundreds of prophets. People weren't always sure what to make of them. Even the terminology used to label them varies. There is the term *ro'eh*, "one who sees," *nabi'*, "one who speaks for," *hōzeh*, also a "seer." There was no single type of prophet just as today there is no single way to be prophetic.

What were the qualifications needed to be a prophet? Today we have strength-finders, brain preference testing, and aptitude measurements. Did the prophets have some innate ability that launched them into their work? Hardly. John Goldingay, analyzing those God called to be prophets, concluded that "there is nothing special about being one through whom [the Lord] speaks. It is not a sign of deep commitment or spirituality or insight."[2] Walter Brueggemann spoke of these same prophets as "uncredentialed" and "without pedigree."[3] Qualifications appear to have been of no interest to Israel's God. Someone is simply chosen to listen and share. The prophets themselves expressed shock, dismay, and uneasiness when summoned by God. Maybe some refused the role; some probably never even heard God calling.

Isolated with No Prospects

In the middle of 1 Kings, the chronicle of monarchs coming and going is interrupted by a little set of stories about Elijah. Like King David, Elijah was at his best when he was weak. Every time he flexed his prophetic muscle, suffering followed. His story begins in the middle of nowhere (1 Kgs 17). Elijah, from Tishbe in Gilead, as obscure as Nazareth, was instructed by God to hide near the Wadi Cherith where he would be fed by ravens. The wadi did what wadis do: it dried up, leaving Elijah not only alone and in hiding but thirsty. Then God sent him to Zarephath, which was a long, arduous journey from the Wadi Cherith, where he met a poor widow with a dying son.

It would be difficult to imagine a more inauspicious, unpromising beginning to a prophetic career. Elijah was alone, had no resources, and his ministry was to the remnants of a fledgling family with no prospects. Is this what biblical leadership is like? Apparently, yes. Elijah was to have compassion on the lowliest, the least, the lost, the very small and very weak, just one mother and her child. And he himself was lonely and hungry. Modern leadership thinks big numbers, metrics, productivity, bang for the buck. But biblical leadership will leave the ninety-nine sheep to seek out the one. Biblical leadership is all compassion. The old rabbinic saying is true: to save one is to save the world.

Bishop Peter Weaver tells a wonderful story of a pastor who almost didn't get to the church one Sunday. Seeing heavy snow out his window, he debated whether to bother braving the elements. His wife urged him to stay bundled in the house: *Surely no one will come.* But he trudged through the snow, and, of course, no one was there. He was about to leave when the door opened, and a man who had not been to church for three years entered. He lived within eyeshot of the sanctuary and said he noticed the pastor had come.

He had been away for so long because his wife had died a terrible death. He was simply not on speaking terms with God and struggled to be in the company of others. He opened up to the pastor, pouring out his heart. They shed tears, embraced, prayed, and then parted ways. Bishop Weaver's assessment of what transpired when only one showed up for worship? "It could not have been more significant if there had been a hundred or a thousand." We might wonder if leadership in small things is more pleasing to God than leadership in large things.

Elijah was lonely. Over time, his loneliness intensified. Facing intense opposition with the queen threatening his life, he repeatedly prayed: "I, even I only, am left" (1 Kgs 18:22, 19:10). Even the little shade he found was lonely: "He sat down under a solitary broom tree" (19:4). Leadership battles loneliness, but every person being led also struggles with loneliness.

Isolation can be withering. Yet doesn't significant transformation in the world usually begin with one solitary soul? There is a terrific TED Talk that features Derek Sivers talking about "How to Start a Movement."[4] Sivers shows a video of a bunch of people lounging on a hillside.

Out of the blue, one guy stands up and starts dancing, flailing about kookily. Gradually people begin to look up and notice. Some ignore him. Others are a little amused by his lunacy. But after a bit, another guy decides, *What the heck—I'll join him.* Similar silly dance moves, just having fun. The two carry on for maybe a minute, and then a third guy joins them. Within seconds, there are two more, then five more, then everybody on that hillside swarms together, dancing, laughing, having a ball.

Sivers's point is that this is how movements begin. The first dancer has to have some guts, a willingness to look ridiculous and not care if anybody actually follows or not. The second guy is hugely important because if he never joins in, the leader would get weary and sit down. The real key is the next guy, since "three's a crowd." With him there's momentum. A tipping point is achieved. After three, there's no reason not to join in.

Vernon Johns preached at Dexter Avenue Baptist in Montgomery about civil rights and was ridiculed by his own people. Then Martin Luther King Jr. spoke up. Then Rosa Parks didn't stand up. Ralph Abernathy, Mother Pollard, John Lewis, and a host of others made it a movement. In the Middle Ages, John Wyclif spoke up and met harsh resistance. But then Martin Luther nailed his theses, and before you knew it, Melanchthon, Calvin, Zwingli, and thousands became the Protestant Reformation. At the birth of any significant movement, the leader is alone. If a vote were taken, she would lose in laughable fashion. Elijah, parched with thirst and desperately depressed, did as the Lord told him, not knowing where he or the Lord's cause would wind up. A leader with zero followers.

A Contest of Wills

Then unexpectedly, out of total obscurity, Elijah found himself standing in the palace before King Ahab and making a smart-alecky remark: "Ahab said to him, 'Is it you, you troubler of Israel?' [Elijah]

53

answered, 'I have not troubled Israel; but you have'" (1 Kgs 18:17-18). A comic-book-like contest was then staged, reminding us of the encounter between David and Goliath. A gigantic crowd of 450 prophets versus lone Elijah on Mount Carmel. As was the case with David, Elijah understood what was at stake: the identity of the true God and the character of that true God. Elijah painted the stakes with black and white clarity: "How long will you go limping with two different opinions? If the LORD is God, follow him; but if Baal, then follow him" (v. 21).

Ahab wasn't irreligious. Like all of Israel, he worshipped Yahweh, the God of Moses. But he (and they!) also dabbled in the worship of Baal—and understandably! The Israelites had moved into the hill country of a strange land. They took up farming, no easy matter on the rocky, terraced slopes. And then there was no rain for a week, two weeks, a month. Their Canaanite neighbors advised them to worship at the sanctuary of Baal, the rain god. At first, the pious, monotheistic Israelites said *No way, we worship one God, Yahweh.* But still no rain. Then one night, a couple of them sneaked off with a modest sacrifice and prayed to Baal for rain. All it took was one shower the next day, and they were hooked. Not to mention Baal's services were entertaining, with something of a sexual edge.

Elijah and his successors railed against this dabbling in the worship of Baal—partly because Baal was not a god at all, partly because that sexual edge verged on the immoral. Furthermore, Canaanite religion implied Canaanite social practices, which was a top-down pyramid arrangement where the poor slavishly served the rich, alien to Israel's egalitarian way. Yahweh was a jealous god, not in the sense of being petty or small-minded. Yahweh loved the people, and knew what would enable them to flourish.

This scenario of competing deities may strike us as prehistoric. But the peril is alive and well today, and leaders bear the responsibility to name our confusion of gods. We worship the Christian God, yes, but then we revere patriotism or pleasure or money as deities who occupy God's space on the altar of our passion. The prosperity gospel; the thin religion that is nothing but me and my goodness; or the vain notion that

God will be my personal assistant, my energy drink, my security blanket: these seemingly innocent blendings lead us far from the heart of the living God and lure us into behaviors and social preferences that are not of God. Once in a while, Christian leaders in the corporate world begin to wonder if their business is a front-and-center display of what truly is idolatry. What do you do once you recognize your work props up a false rival to the true God?

Facing those 450 prophets by himself, Elijah felt some righteous rage rippling through his soul. Chest out, teeth clenched, Elijah taunted the Canaanite prophets laboring so hard to get Baal to rain fire down on the altar: "At noon Elijah mocked them, saying, 'Cry aloud! Surely he is a god; either he is meditating, or he has wandered away, or he is on a journey, or perhaps he is asleep'" (1 Kgs 18:27). Quite a few interpreters suggest that the Hebrew connotes the insulting, embarrassing notion that perhaps Baal is off urinating or having a bowel movement.

What happens next makes us cheer—then shudder. The story claims God acted like a Greek god tossing thunderbolts down to earth. The fire consumed not just the bull on the altar but all the jars of water Elijah had poured on it just to underline his point. As a finishing touch, Elijah slaughtered the 450 prophets of Baal.

Sometimes biblical leaders turn out to be just plain ruthless. Was that lightning really from God? Or merely a bolt of sheer luck just in the nick of time? We hope Rowan Williams is right when he suggests that God doesn't endorse everything in scripture that claims to be of God. Through scripture,

> God is saying, "This is how people heard me, saw me, responded to me; this is the gift I gave them; this is the response they made.... Where are you in this?" If in that story we find accounts of the responses of Israel to God that are shocking or hard to accept, we do not have to work on the assumption that God *likes* those responses.[5]

Indeed, we read of genocide and vengeful slaughtering, as in the case of Elijah on Mount Carmel. Is the counsel for leaders today *Go thou and do likewise*? Williams can't believe God would order such a mass killing because "that would be so hideously at odds with what the biblical story as a whole seems to say about God." Just because biblical people thought they were carrying out God's will, and wrote about it, doesn't mean they were in fact doing God's will. Just because a leader today claims to be in sync with God does not make it so.

As is so often the case, the way the rabbis interpreted this story is quite helpful.[6] Maimonides, in the twelfth century, read this text closely. Taking into account the rest of scripture, he noticed some interesting details. God did not tell Elijah to challenge the Canaanite prophets, and God certainly did not direct Elijah to slaughter them. Prophets are not to intimidate or terrorize others; compulsion and force are not God's ways. Elijah's "zeal" for God was not holy. God was fuming with Elijah afterward, which is why he wound up alone on Mount Horeb. Elijah had to learn the hard way the extreme dangers of religious zealotry. His show of strength impressed but with catastrophic results.

We might linger a moment over the way those prophets of Baal cried out loud to an apparently absent or nonexistent God—and at noon! Jesus, from the cross, the leader of all leaders, cried from the cross, "My God, my God, why have you forsaken me?" (Matt 27:46). He was mocked, just as Ahab's prophets were mocked by Elijah. Onlookers even thought Jesus was pleading for help from, of all people, Elijah. I wonder if we can imagine Jesus in solidarity here not with the boastful Elijah, so zealous for holy victory, but with the false prophets in their forsakenness and then death. Is God's all-enveloping mercy and redemptive power too small for them too? Was God really delighted with Elijah's trouncing of his foes? Isn't God very present with, and merciful toward, those who are terribly wrong and against us when we are sure we are very right?

Exhausted and Disillusioned

The sheer effort to carry out God's will can be exhausting. Elijah's miracle had no lasting impact, and Queen Jezebel swiftly sent out a posse to kill him. He ran for his life. After a hard, hot day of trudging through the wilderness, he cried out, "It is enough!" (1 Kgs 19:4). The Hebrew is not three words and four syllables, as in "It is enough!" With crisp brevity, really nothing more than a grunt, Elijah emitted a yelp, a groan, one word, one syllable only: *rav!* Croaking in exhaustion, burned out: *rav!* His next word was just as abrupt and emphatic; it is just a single syllable even in English: *Now! I've had enough; I want it to end*—Now! So harrowing, this urge toward death—now. Why was he so weary and disillusioned? Was it the vicious hounding from Jezebel, Ahab, and their henchmen? Was it his own hard-headedness? Was God to blame? It was God who got Elijah into this mess in the first place. Leadership grows weary. Where is the blame to be laid? Is it the job? Is it the circumstances? Is it God?

Elijah meandered as far as Mount Horeb, and his arrival there whets our appetite for something marvelous to happen. Moses went up into a cloud on that same mountain and spoke with God face-to-face. We might hope or expect that God would soothe Elijah: offer some rest and relaxation, some reassurance, maybe a sabbatical from his grueling prophetic schedule. But instead, exposed to the elements, Elijah had to withstand a wind storm so strong it broke rocks into pieces, then an earthquake, and then fire, which Elijah had welcomed in his contest with the 450 prophets! But now? First Kings 19:12 reports that the Lord was not in the wind, earthquake, or fire. Then the writer tersely adds, "and after the fire a sound of sheer silence." Older translations rendered this "a still small voice," but the Hebrew indicates there was silence, total, crushing, deafening silence. What kind of response to Elijah's cry was the hollow nothingness of total silence?

There is so much ambiguity in this (and every) silence. Is God refusing to speak? Is it a test? How often do leaders look for some sign, some obvious word, but are greeted with nothing but no word at all? Is it an invitation into something deeper in the heart of God? Mother Teresa said, "God is the friend of silence,"[7] and most great mystics have probed and learned to delight in the quiet that is at the core of God's being. When we listen for God and hear only silence, especially if we are alone, does it feel like loneliness—or solitude? Isn't solitude a razor's edge from loneliness and yet different by light years? Solitude is being quiet, and alone, but with God. If Sabbath is a time to be quiet with God, then perhaps silence is the most tender, restful way God is with us.

The Demand for Justice

Out of that crushing silence, Elijah was pushed right back into the fray at that perilous intersection of politics and religion. Try as we might, we cannot segregate our beliefs about God and our political leanings. Faith is never a private or thinly "spiritual" matter. What we believe about God reveals what we believe about how the world ought to be arranged.

We see the political and social consequences of belief in Israel's God in Elijah's last and ugliest face-off against Ahab and Jezebel. Ahab spotted a vineyard he wanted for a vegetable garden—a trivial hankering for a king with so much power. He was sure it would be simple enough just to pay the owner, Naboth, who had next to nothing, for the property. But Naboth refused to sell. He wasn't holding out for a higher price. In Israel, land was granted to families in perpetuity; God divvied up the land so everyone would have enough. Israel's sense of the meaning and purpose of resources could not be more different from that of the Canaanites and all the other nations, including our own. It did not suit God for a few to get rich while others were diminished. Christian leaders always hold this in mind.

In a laughable scene, Ahab went home having failed to make his purchase, "resentful and sullen" (1 Kgs 21:4), only to be taunted by his overbearing wife, Jezebel: "Do you now govern Israel?" (v. 7). How often does a leader face withering critique from a spouse? Leaving Ahab more resentful and sullen, Jezebel took matters into her own hands. She paid two scoundrels to file false charges against Naboth, and she had him stoned to death as punishment. Christians shiver at this, remembering the trumped-up charges that led to Jesus's crucifixion. The small parcel of land was hers. So it was done in Canaan, Sidon, Babylon, and all other nations. This was justice enough for everyone else.

But not in Israel, and God again did not let this travesty of justice go unchecked. God sent Elijah to expose Jezebel and Ahab, much as Nathan had gone to David for a similar crass, cruel act. Biblical leaders are attentive to signs of injustice. Biblical leaders notice the hidden connections between pious beliefs and social rights and wrongs. Someone has to ask, *Who are the Jezebels? And Ahabs? And Naboths?* Church people might chat in chipper tones about being blessed. But who is disenfranchised by the system that allegedly blesses some but not all? If business is thriving, who is suffering because of it?

Study Questions

1. How can prophetic leadership, which ideally comes from outside an institution, happen from within an institution?

2. Would you agree with Goldingay, that God can speak through someone who has no special commitment, spirituality, or insight?

3. Why is leadership inevitably lonely? And how would a leader cope with or even capitalize on such loneliness?

4. Which gods vie for our attention at the expense of the true God?

5. How do you feel about the suggestion that Elijah heard God incorrectly? And when do leaders think they've heard God but they haven't?

6. Who are the Jezebels, Ahabs, and Naboths of our world? How do we labor for God's justice?

ELISHA

Mentoring and Humility

For many, the best way to survive and to grow as a leader is to find and cultivate an engaged relationship with a mentor. Sometimes, the mentor is the very one who took you by the hand and led you into the very work you're in that sometimes feels like a plague. But the importance of having someone who is wise, who can speak the truth, and who will model faithful leadership cannot be overestimated. And you might hear the calling to become a mentor yourself: what better use of leadership savvy could there be than to invest in someone just coming along? Jonathan Sacks was right: "A good leader creates followers. A great leader creates leaders."[1]

We can think of Elijah as a mentor to Elisha. We don't know much about their interpersonal relationship. In 1 Kings 19 we witness a curious moment. Coming down from the deafening silence on Mount Horeb, Elijah walked by Elisha, whom Elijah evidently did not know and who was out plowing. Elijah threw his mantle over him, which must have come as quite a surprise. Then, even more surprisingly and abruptly, Elisha left his oxen right out in the field and became Elijah's servant—reminiscent of the way some fishermen who had no idea who Jesus was simply dropped everything and traipsed off after him.

Years passed. We can assume Elisha watched Elijah, helped him, learned, questioned, and marveled. Clearly there were other groups of prophets with leaders, functioning like guilds or apprenticeships (2 Kgs 2:3, 4:38). Were there others attached to Elijah? Elisha would eventually have his understudies as well (2 Kgs 4:38, 6:1). No qualifications or credentials were required to become a prophet, but quite a few located mentors. Mentors matter.[2]

The story picks back up not long before Elijah's death, and his strange movements indicate he preferred to go off and die alone (2 Kgs 2). But Elisha would not leave him alone despite Elijah's efforts to shed him like a pesky gnat. Was he sparing Elisha?

Just before a whirlwind swept Elijah up into heaven, Elisha, pitifully, understandably, and bravely, asked the dying Elijah for a "double share" (v. 9) of his power. Elisha had to feel too small, too weak for the task. Did he suspect that, with Elijah gone, he would need not merely the resources he had within himself, or what he had soaked up from Elijah over the years, but an extra dosage? Evidently, that "double share" was forthcoming. Were we to count, we would notice that Elisha doubled—exactly—Elijah's miracle output, sixteen to eight. Great leaders and mentors dream of their successors doing greater things.

Jesus promised the disciples that they would do "greater things." How could anybody top Jesus, much less those weak, uncredentialed, bumbling disciples? Yet they went, and the rest is history. The remarkable narrative in 2 Kings 2 invites us not to trust in ourselves or even to put our abilities to work for God but simply to make a promise, to plunge headlong into continuing what's been started.

The mantle Elijah had thrown on Elisha when they first met was the mantle draped over Elisha's shoulders as Elijah departed. Did it fit? Was it too big? In *The Lord of the Rings*, the wise wizard Gandalf somewhat foolishly left the course of affairs in Middle Earth to the diminutive, fun-loving, timid hobbits.

> "Despair, or folly?" asked Gandalf. "It is not despair, for despair is only for those who see the end beyond all doubt. We do not. It is wisdom to recognize necessity, when all other courses have been weighed, though as folly it may appear to those who cling to false hope. Well, let folly be our cloak, a veil before the eyes of the Enemy!"[3]

What complex feelings stir when a great leader, a wise sage, a stellar saint departs? Is our grief less because we know she or he is with God? Or is our grief heightened because of the sanctity lost? I think of great ones I have known who have died. Fr. Roland Murphy, the brilliant Carmelite Old Testament scholar, my dissertation advisor, and my lifelong mentor, shared much wisdom with me; I never made an important decision without consulting with him. But he did not, as he could not, vouchsafe to me what his dying moments were like or what he saw when the door of this transient life closed and he took the first step on his next journey. He died on the feast day of Elijah—so fitting for a Carmelite and a Hebrew Bible expert! Were there chariots? Or some dimly lit, beautiful silence? We do not know, but we trust, perhaps because we have loved and lost, and harbor in our souls some mysterious confidence that all must be well with someone who lived so well and loved us so well.

Leading Others Humbly into Humility

Nowhere was ancient Israel more at odds with the rest of the world than in its dream and outright demand that leaders be humble. When we look at the pyramids of the pharaohs, and the ziggurats built by the Babylonian kings, we see emblems of pride and power, dedicated to the glory of the pharaohs and kings willing to be dubbed gods walking the earth. Rulers had their names etched on every massive structure, even those their predecessors had built. Contrast their egos to what we read in Numbers 12:3: "Moses was very humble, more so than anyone else on the face of the earth." In all of the Torah, only one person is actually commanded to be humble: the king!

> When he has taken the throne of his kingdom, he shall have a copy of this law written for him.... It shall remain with him and he shall read in it all the days of his life, so that he may learn to fear the LORD... [not] exalting himself above other members of the community. (Deut 17:18-20)

Micah 6:8 says that the Lord requires that we "walk humbly." The posture of the people of God is depicted in the prayer of Psalm 131: "O LORD, my heart is not lifted up, / my eyes are not raised too high" (v. 1). Jesus said to people humbled by the world, "Blessed are the meek" (Matt 5:5). Jesus was meek. His best teachings were about humility. Paul urged his readers, "[Do] not think of yourself more highly than you ought" (Rom 12:3). Faith really is nothing but humility before God. And humility is simply embracing your smallness, your weakness.

Humility is not humiliation. Humility is the liberating truth that I am not God; I am not Atlas hoisting the world on my shoulders; I am not Sisyphus thinking I can push this rock to the top of the hill. One of Winston Churchill's noteworthy *bon mots* came after a colleague was described as a humble man; Churchill retorted, "And he has much to be humble about."[4] We all have much to be humble about, and that's a joyful, freeing confession. The humble are teachable. The humble never try to go it without God, or others. The meek "shall inherit the earth" (Matt 5:5).

Even in the secular world, humility is recognized as essential. Jim Collins's much-touted "Level 5 leader" demonstrates "a compelling modesty, shunning public adulation, never boastful."[5] The humble, not eager for praise, often get some anyway. Thomas Merton provides us with a vision of how lovely that can be: "The humble man receives praise the way a clean window takes the light of the sun. The truer and more intense the light is, the less you see of the glass."[6]

The Bible narrates the humbling of the powerful, and we even read some enchanting instances where a holy leader manages to elicit humility in another powerful person. Consider Naaman, who was a mighty man of valor. "But"—and there's always a *but*—"he was a leper" (2 Kgs 5:1 RSV). We can be sure he privately sought help from great healers. But it was a little girl, a slave who had come to him in the spoils of war, who knew to send him to Elisha, a modest prophet in a modest place. Naaman rumbled up to Elisha's house with his chariot pulled by steeds, surrounded by his entourage. His soldier knocked on the door; Elisha did not even come out.

He sent this mighty warrior a terse message: "Wash in the Jordan seven times" (v. 10). Naaman was appalled by this affront. Elisha somehow knew Naaman needed to be healed not merely of his leprosy but of his pridefulness. Elisha showed Naaman the way to weakness. He refused to feed Naaman's ego. He prescribed humbling actions: dipping oneself in a muddy no-account creek. Naaman was healed, and the writer tells us that when he stepped up onto the bank, drenched with water, "his flesh was restored like the flesh of a young boy" (v. 14). Didn't the greatest leader ever indicate that we must become like children, small and weak?

How can a leader introduce others to the way of humility? Not by humiliating the other; too many leaders think the best way to prod followers is by shaming. Never—at least not in God's kingdom. Perhaps humble leaders simply refuse to hide their own weaknesses from themselves or others. Perhaps we engage in humbling actions as an example, and then walk alongside others on their journey toward humility. It always involves the leader understanding that weakness, so feared in the world, is a holy place where God lives with us. Limitations, which we vainly assume we can overcome, are built into us so we will know the tender mercy of God and discover community and hope in God.

Study Questions

1. When have you seen a great leader who creates leaders? How was it done?

2. Who has been a mentor to you, in religious life or in secular life?

3. Why is humility so important to leadership? And why do we not then seek leaders who are humble?

4. How is weakness a holy place where God lives in us?

MICAIAH

Yes-Men versus Truth-Tellers

Earlier, we saw Nathan fulfilling the prophetic role in his confrontation with David (2 Sam 12). David thought he had covered up the tawdry Bathsheba caper. But God knew, and God didn't leave things unaddressed. Nathan was known to David and trusted by him—perhaps because of his courage and love and perhaps because he was familiar with Nathan's wise tactics. Instead of a shrill denunciation, Nathan simply told a story: the parable of the man who stole another man's sheep. Think of leaders you know, or historic figures like Abraham Lincoln or Ronald Reagan, with that uncanny ability to tell a story that defuses tension or enlightens cheerfully. What better way to bring God's truth to one in power? David's humility, his weakness in the face of this prophet, was impressive. David could have had Nathan killed as easily as he had dispatched Uriah. But instead, David was ashamed, mortified, and repented. Not all kings would respond so well.

A little over a century later, a dramatic encounter unfolded that tells us a lot about prophetic leadership. King Ahab (yes, that nasty one married to Jezebel) of the northern kingdom of Israel tried to lure King Jehoshaphat (yes, the one with the humble prayer) of the southern kingdom into an alliance to launch an attack on Ramoth-gilead, a strategic piece of land that promised heightened security and increased revenues to Ahab's realm. Jehoshaphat was eager to be supportive, but suggested they ask a prophet for a word from the Lord. Ahab summoned four hundred prophets to ask, "Shall I go to battle against Ramoth-gilead?" (1 Kgs 22:6). With one voice, all four hundred said, "Go up; for the Lord will give it into the hand of the king."

But Jehoshaphat, with either terrific intuition or a contrarian mindset, asked if there were any other prophets to consult. Ahab admitted, "There is still one other by whom we may inquire of the Lord, Micaiah son of Imlah; but I hate him, for he never prophesies anything favorable about me" (v. 8). Predictably, Micaiah prophesied doom. After Ahab whispered an "I told you so" to Jehoshaphat, a court official named Zedekiah slapped Micaiah on the cheek, upbraided him, and threw him in jail. Taking four hundred to one as more than sufficient support, Ahab plunged headlong into the ill-advised skirmish. He did disguise himself—revealing his sneaking suspicion that Micaiah may actually have heard from God. His costume notwithstanding, a stray arrow aimed at someone else struck him in the lone vulnerable spot between armor and breastplate, and he died.

Whatever They Want to Hear

There are always false prophets who seem clever or even claim to speak for God but are nothing more than yes-men for the powers that be. The philosopher Harry Frankfurt defined *bullshit* not as lying, but as saying whatever the listener wants to hear.[1] Those in power (and also regular people) inevitably have viewpoints and fantasies they wish were of God, and they very much want to hear smooth words that reinforce their biases. Even scripture itself can be misused. Charles Schulz penned a humorous cartoon I keep in my office in which a young man asks his friend to leave him alone, as he's busy hunting down a Bible verse to back up one of his preconceived notions. How many wars and foolish endeavors have been blessed by religious leaders parroting back to politicians exactly what they wanted to hear? How often do we all listen for and mutter an *Amen* when some pious preacher or writer wraps a supportive cloak of words around our pet biases and vain wishes? How many dumb decisions have been made because trusted advisers wanted to please?

Aristotle suggested that the opposite of a friend is a flatterer. In our culture we love to hear happy things. Chris Lowney, assessing effective leadership, writes that "leaders make themselves and others comfortable in a changing world."[2] Prophetic leadership, at least in Bible times, made themselves and others profoundly uncomfortable. The biblical prophets, like Micaiah, stood as haunting question marks against all assumptions, toppling the house of cards, forcing radical reconsideration not just of whether to go into battle with Ramoth-gilead but of the entire culture. Ahab's kingdom bristled with injustice and unholiness long before his ill-fated foray across the border. In assessing how to run a business, Patrick Lencioni shows how simple inquiry, an openness to hard questions, confession and truth-telling, is pivotal; he speaks of "the willingness of people to abandon their pride and their fear, to sacrifice their egos for the collective good of the team."[3] The prophets are more than willing to help.

Deep inside, most of us fret over the possibility that our preconceived notions, our settled assumptions, are a bit skewed, or perhaps entirely bankrupt, loath as we may be to admit it. Anne Lamott famously said, "If you want to make God laugh, tell her your plans."[4] In his commentary on our 1 Kings 22 passage, Peter Leithart put it more strongly: "The word of Yahweh does not affirm us in our plans. It challenges our plans, confronts them, undoes them."[5] No single prophetic word was truer than that succinct utterance, "My thoughts are not your thoughts, / nor are your ways my ways, says the LORD" (Isa 55:8).

Micaiah, like all prophets, had much courage and got himself physically abused and thrown in the slammer. There is a cost to prophetic leadership—although it is important to consider whether the suffering a leader might bear is really due to being so bold and in sync with God or if the leader has simply been offensive, obnoxious, and not at all in tune with God's way. Four hundred to one leaves you feeling pretty lonely. How did Imlah, Micaiah's father, feel about all this? We might admire a leader's splendid isolation, but isolation is isolation. And the impact on others is grievous, as we will see.

So as not to skate over the details of 1 Kings 22 too swiftly, it is worth noting that the oracle of the four hundred was not as smashingly supportive as we might suppose. If we slow down and read carefully, we realize their words were ambiguous. They said, "Go up; for the LORD will give it into the hand of the king" (v. 6). Give *it*—but what? And into the hand of the king—but *which* king? Maybe this is like one of those haunting oracles from Greek tragedies, whose ambiguity reveals what the listener is determined to do no matter what. Maybe these yes-men were hedging their bets, playing it safe, leaving some wiggle room if Ahab lost and came back for an accounting. Leithart shrewdly observes, "For prophets, ambiguity lends a great deal of job security"[6]—and wobbly job security makes cowards of us all.

When we ponder this story we find ourselves perched between the ever-present possibilities of true and false prophecies. How would a listener discern which message is of God? Two options (and it could be the awful "lesser of two evils" quandary or two happy options) present themselves without clarity on which way to go. How does a faithful leader choose? In this case, the outcome of the battle swiftly vindicated Micaiah. Let's fast-forward 250 years to a similar quandary involving the prophet Jeremiah.

Study Questions

1. Why do leaders listen to the yes-people, and why are they so resistant to truth-tellers?

2. What are the costs of truth-telling for the truth-tellers?

3. How can we become the kind of people eager to hear hard truths?

4. How do we discern which messages are of God and which only pretend to be so, however nobly intended?

JEREMIAH

Courage and Its Costs

Jeremiah 27–28 narrates a dramatic standoff between Jeremiah and Hananiah. Early in King Zedekiah's reign, when Jerusalem was hanging by a thread and would soon be reduced to rubble, God instructed Jeremiah to fashion straps and yoke bars and wear them around his neck (Jer 27). The king and people, according to Jeremiah, were to submit to Nebuchadnezzar of Babylon for they would very soon find themselves in harsh servitude to the Babylonians. Obviously, not quite what Zedekiah and the people had hoped to hear.

In strode another prophet, Hananiah, from Gibeon, who declared, "Thus says the LORD of hosts, the God of Israel: I have broken the yoke of the king of Babylon" (Jer 28:2) and that all would be restored in just a few months. Then with a show of fury, Hananiah grabbed the yoke from Jeremiah's neck and broke it. We can imagine the cheers from the crowd and the smirk on King Zedekiah's face. Strong stuff.

Jeremiah had to look like a weakling. He went away for a while but then returned and told Hananiah, "The LORD has not sent you, and you made this people trust a lie" (v. 15). And then, without saying God caused it, but implying divine judgment, the text reads, "In that same year . . . the prophet Hananiah died" (v. 17).

But who could leap to the conclusion that those who truly speak the Lord's word live and those who don't die? In our experience, and if history teaches us anything, the opposite seems to hold. How many martyrs suffered cruelty for speaking truth? How often do we withhold truth, or not bother to notice it, as the costs of truth-telling are so high? "Why do the wicked prosper?" (Job 21:7 NLT).

This story seems to suggest that whoever predicts the future correctly is the true prophet. But biblical prophecy isn't primarily prediction. The prophets didn't gaze into their crystal balls to forecast events far in the future. They spoke God's word to real people in real situations. The ultimate truth of a prophet's preaching isn't *Do his predictions actually happen?* But rather *How clearly in the light of God's law and justice does the prophet diagnose what is going on and what the likely consequences will be?* Besides, who can wait around to see what comes true and what doesn't? You hear a prophetic word, or conflicting prophetic words, and you have to make a decision now. Which way to go? What strategy to pursue?

Israel's sacred stories, laws, and theology pulsated with both words of judgment and words of hope, razor sharp critique, and warm, maternal solace. Jeremiah uttered words of judgment while Hananiah spoke of hope and comfort. Was Hananiah wrong? God's way *is* one of hope and comfort after all. The problem apparently was that Hananiah was offering comfort when the times required repentance. John Goldingay is right: "A true prophet is someone who knows what time it is."[1] Finely tuned discernment and a knack for overhearing the heart of God are required of leaders to know what time it is—the hour to afflict the comfortable or the hour to comfort the afflicted.

It's humbling to realize how often our timing is off. When does a leader push hard? And when does that same leader relax the pressure and leave room for mercy? Maybe if a leader can cultivate a heart that is close to God's heart the timing will improve. After all, wrath and mercy are not really divergent moods within God, as if some pendulum swings and God is angry now but tender then. Wrath and mercy, judgment and comfort are one in God. Jesus always knew when to be firm and when to be tender and in such a way that his tenderness seemed firm and his firmness nothing but mercy.

The Costs of Leadership

Even if there were no opposition or anger to deal with, just standing in the breach, having to make tough, uncertain decisions and questioned discernments, exacts a toll on anyone who would be a prophetic leader. Elijah was threatened, mocked, and hounded, and wound up alone and severely depressed. We do not know what Nathan's personal life was like, but it cannot have been comfortable living near David's palace after exposing the king's moral shortcomings. A century after Elijah, Hosea's wife, Gomer, was unfaithful, and it is not entirely clear if the text is to be taken at face value: that God actually ordered him to marry a prostitute or if Gomer slept around later. Either way, his experience of her infidelity taught him the hard lesson he then shared with the people about their infidelity to the Lord; his agony and shame must have been shattering.

More than any other prophet, Jeremiah provides us with a harrowing yet hopeful glimpse into his private darkness. His words of judgment and warning were unwanted and unheeded by the people. His language and imagery—or were they God's?—were far from subtle or gentle. The people were compared to whores, to a gangly young camel in heat, to terrorists. Yet we don't get the feel that he was an angry, raging street preacher. What was his tone of voice? Did he shout and bellow in stern judgment? Or was he more plaintive? Jeremiah wept over his people's waywardness and over their dogged unwillingness to turn toward life (Jer 9:1). How do leaders who must speak hard words let the audience know they simultaneously shed tears for them? That it truly is a lover's quarrel?

The people to whom he preached weren't hookers or the tawdry. They were fine, upstanding people who showed up at the temple regularly for prayers and sacrifice (Jer 7, 26). Many were priests and prophets themselves. They were blind to their own lunacy, deaf to their twisted priorities. The very fact that they were sure they were righteous only heightened the ferocity of their response.

The burden of delivering these castigating indictments of the people for their idolatry, injustice, immorality, and foolishness was crushing. We hear no words of appreciation from Jeremiah's listeners. We do know he was treated harshly by kings, other prophets, the rabble, and even his own family. The few friends he had abandoned him. The priest, Pashur, struck him and put him in the stockade (Jer 20:1-2). Like Paul, Martin Luther King Jr., and a host of prophetic leaders, he was in and out of jail.

Jeremiah's worst imprisonment though might have been within himself—and he felt like God was his jailer. Rippling with intense emotion, Jeremiah cried out in his despair not merely pleading with God for help but actually blaming God for his troubles. "O LORD, you have enticed me... / you have overpowered me" (Jer 20:7). Jeremiah was called by God, which sounds deeply spiritual. But for the agony it brought upon him, Jeremiah came to see that calling as an *enticement*, a word with a more sinister connotation than *calling*. "I have become a laughingstock all day long; / everyone mocks me.... / For the word of the LORD has become for me / a reproach and derision all day long" (vv. 7-8).

His mood plummeted to even darker places. "Cursed be the day on / which I was born! / The day when my mother bore me, / let it not be blessed! / Cursed be the man / who brought the news to my father, saying, / 'A child is born to you, a son'" (vv. 14-15). Jack Lundbom reminds us of how frequent and poignant this death-wish is: from Job to Hamlet to Hector's wife, Andromache.[2] For Jeremiah it's tantamount to blasphemy to wish to undermine the creator's gift of life, God's determination that life should be. And what a shocking reversal from the way Jeremiah understood his vocation! It was in his mother's womb that Jeremiah was called by God (1:5), but once he was older, he regretted that her womb was not his grave (20:17).

Despising his own birth, Jeremiah never married or had children (16:2), so he was granted no domestic respite from his embattled professional life. Having been called to this vocation when he was just an adolescent, he never enjoyed a sunny season of youthful exploration.

But Jeremiah couldn't hold back. In the same breath with which he lamented his fate, he spoke of unsuccessfully trying to quit: "Within me there is something like a burning fire / shut up in my bones; / I am weary with holding it in, / and I cannot" (20:9).

An Emotionally Healthy Spirituality

If we ponder Jeremiah's immense courage and resilience along with his sheer misery and sorrow, we cannot be sure what it all means for leadership today. We live in a profoundly distressed world that requires leaders with mountains of courage and the will to stick it out through an onslaught of difficulty. And yet we have seen many of our finest, most effective, and desperately needed leaders melt down under the pressure. Their bodies can't sustain the stress; they self-medicate; their families are fractured. How do leaders discern when to press on like Jeremiah or back off for a season, get into therapy, take a sabbatical, or change positions?

Peter Scazzero minted a wonderful program for Christian laity and leaders in and out of the church called "Emotionally Healthy Spirituality."[3] His premise is that we can engage in service to God with abandon, and in a way that earns much popularity, but is unhealthy and theologically unsound. There are spiritually and physically healthy ways to serve God over the long haul: dealing honestly with vulnerability, recognizing and affirming our limits, observing Sabbath, trusting that it is God—not the dint of human effort—who will achieve the kingdom. *Are you weak enough to lead?* is the question.

If the prophets were obsessed with truth, then we might ponder what Jean Vanier, in his theologically robust and spiritually profound book on leadership, *Community and Growth*, suggests:

> To accept our weaknesses and those of others is the very opposite of sloppy complacency. It is essentially a concern for truth, so that we do not live in illusion but can grow from where we are and not from where we want to be or where others want us to be.[4]

Jeremiah owned his weakness, right out in the open for everyone to see. He didn't see his weakness as a problem to be fixed. He just was weak—and as the weak one, he led.

We cannot know where Jeremiah, Hosea, or Elijah might fit along this spectrum from unhealthy to healthy. What we can be sure of is that leadership of all sorts takes a toll on the leader and those who love the leader. How we cope with that toll, and whether there can be redemption through it all, is an open question.

Study Questions

1. If the true prophet "knows what time it is," how do we know if it's time for judgment or hope?

2. When has someone been crushed, inwardly or by outward forces, for being God's messenger?

3. If we are unhappy with or disappointed in God, is it because God didn't do what we wanted or because we did what God wanted?

4. How do leaders strike a balance between serving God zealously and yet maintaining appropriate boundaries and Sabbath-observance?

5. What do you think of Vanier's belief that weakness is the opposite of complacency?

AMOS, SECOND ISAIAH

Judgment and Redemption

The Bible provides us with the words of many other prophets. But we know little about their lives. As the words they conveyed from God grew in importance, the biographical dramas of their lives receded into the background. At some point, leaders begin to understand this principle: it is the message, the product, the direction that matters, not the leader's charisma, brilliance, or charm. A cardinal principle of Jim Collins's *Good to Great* is that leadership does not and should not hinge on a strong, larger-than-life personality being in charge.

Amos was the first prophet, chronologically and alphabetically, with a book in his name. We know a bit about him. He was a herdsman (which implies material success) from Tekoa in the south. He had the nerve, or the divine compulsion, to venture into the north and offer a strident critique of a culture that was prospering. With the pungent disclaimer, "I am no prophet, nor a prophet's son" (Amos 7:14), he distanced himself from the professional prophets who spoke only soothing, supportive words of congratulation to those profiting from injustice and making a sham of piety.

His preaching began well, at least to his listeners. He chided their neighbors, Damascus, Gaza, Tyre, Edom, the Ammonites, Moabites, and then the dreaded Judeans—his own people! We can imagine raucous applause as he spoke God's judgment on Israel's neighbors, zigzagging all over the map. They did not notice he was spinning a web over them in the middle. As if circling in for the kill, he turned his gaze on Israel, dubbing them the guiltiest of the guilty. Leaders who analyze what is out of kilter always need to find this delicate balance between whether to find fault out there or in here. As Christians who understand human nature and the fallen world in which we live, we know it is always both, and there is some artful strategy to owning brokenness not just in here or out there but in both. Perhaps we counter Amos and begin in here instead of casting blame out there. Jesus spoke of the impossibility of retrieving a speck from someone else's eye when a big log is lodged in your own (Matt 7:3).

Amos wasn't done. He spoke words of *Woe!* to "those who are at ease... / who feel secure.... / Who lie on beds of ivory... / who drink wine... / but are not grieved over the ruin" of the poor and disenfranchised (Amos 6:1-6). With startling rudeness, he called the rich women "you cows of Bashan... / who oppress the poor, who crush the needy" (4:1). Imagine their horror. Their husbands surely leapt to their defense, declaring they had earned their money by hard work and smart decision-making and that the poor should fend for themselves. The prophetic leader dares to discern connections between the prosperity of some and the poverty of others. Whether name-calling is a proper strategy is another question.

The people reacted by pointing out they never missed worship and offered even better music and more sumptuous sacrifices than if they had been poorer. Amos was unimpressed—or we should say he overheard God being unimpressed:

I hate, I despise your festivals,
     and I take no delight in your solemn assemblies.
Even though you offer me your burnt offerings
. . . .
     I will not accept them;

76

. . . .
Take away from me the noise of your songs;
    I will not listen to the melody of your harps.
But let justice roll down like waters,
    and righteousness like an ever-flowing stream. (5:21-24)

This passage should make us shudder. Could it be that God, given the myriad of ways our lives are out of sync with God's way, finds our organ playing, praise songs, prayers, and sermons to be just so much annoying racket? Christian leaders are humbled by the dissonance and try to join hands with others to seek out deeper continuities between what we say and do in church and how we actually live in the places where we work, play, live, and learn.

The rest of the prophetic books are of course worthy reads. Isaiah spoke truth to power, and evidently as an insider. He was educated and of some means, enjoying ready access to the royal courts. Talk about a prophetic leader's impact on his family: God instructed him to give his children names that illustrated impending doom for the nation. Think of poor little Maher-shalal-hash-baz ("the spoil speeds, the prey hastens" [Isa 8:1]) and Shear-jashub ("a remnant shall return" [Isa 7:3]) being picked on by other little boys.

We have touched on Hosea's unfortunate marriage to Gomer. Somehow through those tears he articulated what may be the most tender message of God's love in all of scripture. Habakkuk, an obscure prophet with a correspondingly small book written during Israel's weakest days, has bragging rights for uttering the most important verse cited in the entire New Testament: "The righteous live by faith" (Hab 2:4; see Rom 1:17, Gal 3:11). A rollicking good film could be made about Ezekiel: his visions verged on the psychedelic; his symbolic actions (shaving in public, getting sunburned on one side, attacking a brick) were the stuff of lunacy. Jonah, the antileader, fled in the opposite direction from God's call, only to be imprisoned and thereby saved in the belly of a fish; once he reluctantly did what God asked of him, he still pouted. The rest of the prophets, Joel, Obadiah, Micah, Nahum, Zephaniah, Haggai,

Zechariah, Malachi, each had a peculiar, well-targeted message for God's people, but we know nothing about them as people.

Redemption through Suffering

The best place to conclude our exploration of prophetic leadership will be with the eloquent, poetic, moving, and theologically profound words of the prophet we call "Second Isaiah." During those bleakest days when Jerusalem had been reduced to rubble and the people were clinging to life in Babylonian exile, this prophet revived the old prophecies of Isaiah and applied them to this dark age. Goldingay said "a true prophet is someone who knows what time it is."[1] It was time for some hope, time for a miracle, time for redemption, time to return home. "Comfort, O comfort my people, / says your God. / Speak tenderly to Jerusalem / and cry to her / that she has served her term.... / In the wilderness prepare the way of the LORD" (Isa 40:1-3).

What is new and haunting in Second Isaiah's marvelous words is that we get a clear glimpse that this prophet not only delivered God's hopeful word and suffered greatly for it—but also that his suffering wasn't just something to be weathered. Warren Bennis and Robert Thomas speak of "hardiness" in leaders as "the perseverance and toughness that enable people to emerge from devastating circumstances without losing hope."[2] In the pages of Isaiah 40–55 though, we witness a moment when suffering wasn't just something to be weathered or a harrowing through which there might be learning or growth. There was, at least in this prophet's case, something redemptive about suffering.

We are familiar with those words we read on Good Friday, which appear to portray the agonies of Christ on the cross:

> He was despised and rejected by others;
>   a man of suffering, who acquainted with infirmity.
> . . . .
> He was wounded for our transgressions,

crushed for our iniquities;
. . . .
He was oppressed, and was afflicted,
    yet he did not open his mouth. (Isa 53:3, 5, 7)

But these were not crystal ball glimpses of Jesus centuries in advance of his crucifixion. If we back up a bit, we find these words from the same writer:

The Lord God has opened my ear;
    and I was not rebellious
    I did not turn backward.
I gave my back to those who struck me. (Isa 50:5-6)

Scholars rightly understand these enigmatic "suffering servant" passages in this way: Israel still bore the role of the Lord's servant, by whom the Lord would save the world, even in their weakened state, stranded in Babylonian exile. God called this prophet, whose words we now read, to lead them. He was ridiculed, scoffed at, and physically attacked, paying a high price for ministering to them. He wasn't hardy; he was weak. He suffered at their hands but also *with* them.

In time, the notion dawned on him and others that his suffering was not merely heroic or pitiful. Beyond all that, he was actually suffering *for* them—that God somehow was bringing healing even out of the abuse taken by this one who stood up to lead the people back to their laughable but marvelous calling to be the chosen people to bring redemption to all nations.[3] For the first time, we hear what will echo through the hills around Jerusalem when Jesus was crucified and then in the shed blood of holy martyrs through the centuries. Redemption can and does come through suffering.

On a much more modest but still significant scale, leaders today can find healing and redemption in their suffering, in their wounds. Henri Nouwen popularized the notion of "the wounded healer" a generation ago.[4] I can echo his thoughts, for I know that my woundedness is not something I've overcome or that God has fixed. Rather, my woundedness is the place where God has spoken to me, called me, and used me. If I have been of any benefit to anyone as a leader, it is not because I am smart, or hard-working, or well-read. It is my weakest weakness, the broken place in me: this is where the grace and power of God does something miraculous—for the healing not of me but of those around me, the church itself, and even the world.

The redemption of the world has always been God's project, and so we turn all the way back to the beginning to attend to the oldest stories of how we lead and mislead, struggle and then survive, and discover what God is doing in and through our weakness.

Study Questions

1. Why is it hard to remember to begin cleaning up the world at home instead of finding fault out there somewhere?

2. How do you feel about Amos's bad news—that God may well be annoyed by our worship?

3. When have you seen or experienced suffering that proved to be redemptive?

4. Why is it that the wounded healer is able to help, not by having overcome woundedness but simply by being one who is wounded?

GENESIS

Responsibility and Big Plans

W hen we delve into the mists of prehistory, with the Bible's familiar, charming, and still puzzling passages in early Genesis, we certainly don't see any kind of institutional or even large group leading. The first people, those prototypical people whom we all resemble, live in a seemingly simpler yet more dangerous world and always in relationships with others—which for them is where the leading happens.

What feels even more prehistoric is 1 Timothy 2:14, which finds fault with Eve's leading (or *mis*leading) Adam. Both were misled by the serpent. It seems that, from the very beginning, we are people who get misled, and we all mislead; we get each other into trouble.

When confronted by God about the fruit, Adam blamed Eve. Eve blamed the serpent. Both denied responsibility. Since failure to take responsibility is failure of leadership, Adam and Eve demonstrate how failure of leadership is deeply rooted in the very essence of human existence.

God, who could have guessed how things would pan out, had entrusted Adam, Eve, and the rest of us with "dominion," the care for and stewardship of the earth. Even after Adam and Eve shook off responsibility, God didn't take this dominion back from them. They still had the huge responsibility of caring for God's world. God is quite clearly a large-minded, risk-taking, benevolent, and generous leader.

The reader of Genesis can only imagine God's heartbreak as this story unfolds. Cain, the first child, and very strong, was knotted up with jealousy, and in a fit of rage killed his younger and much weaker brother Abel. Can we imagine the horror of Adam and Eve, asking the agonizing question so many parents ask: *What did we do wrong?*

Jonathan Sacks points out that while Adam and Even denied personal responsibility, Cain denied moral responsibility.[1] "Am I my brother's keeper?" (Gen 4:9). Cain must have assumed the answer was *No*. If Darwin was right, that human existence is nothing but a struggle to survive where the strong get ahead, then moral responsibility for others is a fiction. If God is bothered by Darwin's theory of evolution, it's over this survival of the fittest and the idea that it's natural for the weak just to get squashed.

The absence of good leadership continued even with the ultra-righteous Noah. We don't usually fault him simply because no one else joined him on the ark. Sometimes, no matter how visionary or persuasive the leader, nobody follows. But Sacks pieces things together in an intriguing way: "It is reasonable to assume that these two facts—Noah's righteousness and his lack of influence on his contemporaries—are intimately related. Noah preserved his virtue by separating himself from his environment."[2]

The righteous can be so strong that they insulate themselves from others, minimize personal risk, but thereby forsake opportunities for influence. Sacks goes on to explain how Jewish rabbis through the ages spoke of Noah as "a righteous man in a fur coat."[3] On a cold night, you can wear a coat and keep yourself warm, or you can build a fire and make yourself and others warm.

Noah, who for so much of his life was so holy, stumbled later in life when he was found by his sons to be unclothed and drunk. The story only got worse from there. In a seemingly unstoppable tailspin, humanity led itself to build a tower in Babel. We can be sure the architect and chief engineers were lauded for their achievement. But the tower was not of God and led to the splintering of peoples and tension and misunderstanding among nations.

The Power of One

To save this fledgling world, according to the Bible's startling plot, God zoomed in on just one individual. Abraham could be dubbed the most important human ever if we lionize him as the forefather of Jews, Christians, and Muslims. But he was hardly a leader of men and women. What he did, as an example and inspiration to people like Paul or the Gospel writers or saints or you and me, was that he was willing to go; he did not know where—just wherever God told him to go. His over-the-top faith has thrilled and puzzled the faithful of all religions, but he had his issues, and we don't envision him as a leader, *per se*.

Same for his grandson Jacob, who misled his parents and brother, whose favoritism as a father spawned violence among his sons, and whose most exemplary moment was when he managed to eke out a draw in an all-night wrestling match with—well—with whom? God? An angel? An attacker? Sacks offers some wisdom here, which would raise an eyebrow from the author of the text itself and yet is of value:

> People must wrestle with themselves as Jacob did on that fateful night, throwing off the person they might like to be but are not; they must accept that some people will like them and what they stand for while others will not; they must understand that it is better to seek the respect of some than the popularity of all. This may involve a lifetime of struggle, but the outcome is an immense strength. No one is stronger than the person who knows who and what he is.[4]

What we can say about Jacob, his wives and sons, his father, his grandparents, and even Noah in his fur coat is that they were part of something far larger than the bit parts they played. Their lives, while long and fascinating, rich and complex, were temporary roles played in the worldwide drama of God's redemptive plan for all of creation. Quite a few leadership books have quoted Daniel Burnham, the architect who designed urban plans for Chicago and Manila and built the Flatiron Building in New York and the massive World Exposition in Chicago in 1893:

Make no little plans. They have no magic to stir men's blood and probably themselves will not be realized. Make big plans; aim high in hope and work, remembering that a noble, logical diagram once recorded will never die, but long after we are gone will be a living thing, asserting itself with ever-growing insistency.[5]

Abraham made no big plans. But God shared with him some mind-boggling plans: "I will make of you a great nation, and I will...make your name great....And in you all the families of the earth shall be blessed" (Gen 12:2-3). Abraham must have been flabbergasted. His was not to plan but simply to move forward, stage by stage, into an unmapped future just wherever God was inviting him to go.

Theologically, we can always be sure that God makes no little plans. God's plans are bigger than big; they are all-encompassing, and God's plans will never be foiled. My plan is to find our small place within this all-enveloping movement that is the realization of God's reign. Leaders in church, at home, and in the working world reminds us we are part of this larger adventure.

Joseph's Rise and Reconciliation

Then, like a brilliant, bright flare enlightening the night sky just in time to rescue passengers on a sinking ship, out of the morass of failed individuals and dysfunctional, fallen humanity, a leader for all the ages emerged. Joseph, the apple of Jacob's eye, the target of intense loathing by his jealous brothers, a prisoner and then an alien in Egypt: Joseph led pharaohs and his estranged brothers; he led the most important nation on earth during an intense crisis; and even today he leads us with his consummate demonstration of what forgiveness, reconciliation, determination, healing, and hope look like.

The story could not be more riveting or profound. Of all his sons, Jacob loved Joseph best because his deepest affection was for Joseph's mother, Rachel, and not the other mothers of his other boys. Jacob dressed this son, not in an "amazing technicolor dreamcoat" (as in the Andrew Lloyd Webber musical) but (as the Hebrew puts it) in "long sleeves." The other brothers wore short sleeves, which meant their labor was in the fields, in the heat, where briars would get tangled in long sleeves. Joseph was established in the house with those long sleeves in a position of comfort and power over the brothers.

And then he dreamed his dream of their submission to him. Joseph wasn't the kind of dreamer we value today, like Martin Luther King Jr. and his dream of an integrated society, or Steve Jobs and his dream of internet connectivity at your fingertips. Joseph's dream was one God gave him, revealing what the future would hold. The dream must have encouraged Joseph as he must have suffered bouts of fear and darkness in the face of his older brothers' menacing glares and harsh words.

Finally they acted on their rage. They almost killed him, then sold him into abject slavery. Then they crushed their father's heart by showing him Joseph's bloodied long sleeves. Joseph was not undone by circumstance. He not only survived but rose to a place of prominence in Egypt and did so more than once. Should we admire his never-give-up toughness? Or his moral compass—refusing to be seduced by Potiphar's wife? The Bible gives credit where credit is due: "The LORD was with Joseph" (Gen 39:2), a declaration repeated at every turning point in Joseph's blockbuster-worthy life and career. Joseph had brains, courage, and some mix of God's blessing and sheer luck, which the brothers back home didn't have. Evidently, he was at his best when he was at his weakest and most vulnerable.

Years passed. A famine compelled the brothers to go down to Egypt, the breadbasket of the world. In a stunning plot twist, it was Joseph from whom they had to ask for food. He would give them far, far more. Naturally they didn't recognize him, but he recognized them. After dallying with them a bit, he dismissed his entourage from the room, let loose long-pent-up emotions, gathered himself, dried his tears, and revealed his secret: "I am your brother, Joseph" (45:4).

The brothers had to be stricken with shock, horror, guilt, trepidation, remorse. But how did Joseph deal with those who had treated him and his father so cruelly? His words must have taken light years to sink in: "Do not be distressed, or angry with yourselves, because you sold me here; for God sent me before you to preserve life" (v. 5). Even after the glorious reunion with his father, and then even after Jacob's death, Joseph said the most remarkable thing: "Do not be afraid!... Even though you intended to do harm to me, God intended it for good, in order to preserve a numerous people" (50:19-20). Joseph forgave; he cast their common, broken life into the hands of God's larger intentions. Isn't forgiveness a noble kind of weakness, a refusal to assert strength?

Notice the brothers weren't given a "second chance," another crack at getting it right. They never got it right; they never made up for what they had done. God did not depend on any attitude change among the brothers. God quite simply used the evil they perpetrated and transformed it into good.

Not that God caused them to do evil: God did not make them sell their brother or break their father's heart. But God gathered up their misdeeds, the broken will of God, and pieced it all together for God's good purpose. Joseph's leadership was defined by seeing, understanding, and then articulating this. He brought healing to the fractured family and food to a hungry world—or rather, his leading was God's imperceivable, mysterious use of his life and then his awed witness to it.

Faithful leaders try to develop special antennae to detect the way God's saving work is concealed in even the most worldly, unfortunate, untoward circumstances. Maybe some lucky leaders are natively equipped this way. The leader has the humble vision to bear witness to God's larger pattern of work, of how God uses our mistakes—and not only that but then also the way God never rests until we come to reconciliation. Leadership experts Ron Heifetz and Donald Laurie speak of the need for leaders who climb up into the "balcony" and see larger patterns in the workplace.[6] Joseph was caught up far higher than the balcony; he was granted a view from heaven itself.

Claus Westermann wisely noticed that God did not merely use the evil of the brothers; God could have done that without the brothers ever meeting up with Joseph. No, "God's plan is to bring the evil devised by the brothers to good in such a way that there can be forgiveness."[7] The holiest leaders will be the ones who wait for and yearn restlessly for opportunities not only for good to dawn but for fractured relationships to be healed. We don't stamp out evil so much as dare to convert it. Joseph's exemplary leadership redeemed not only his people but also the Egyptian empire, an alien and increasingly hostile place. It is there we meet Moses.

Study Questions

1. Adam and Eve demonstrate our inherent tendency to be misled. How do leaders, and followers, account for and remedy this?

2. Is leadership taking responsibility? What is the difference between personal and moral responsibility?

3. Were the rabbis correct to speak of Noah as "the man in the fur coat"? Have you seen a leader who is amazing—but doesn't really lead anybody?

4. Why is it hard to see how we are part of God's larger work in the world? Are our plans often too small?

5. How do you feel about Joseph's story, and the way God brought good out of evil? Why is it hard to detect God's hidden plot?

6. Bringing reconciliation to broken relationships is hard, but crucial in leadership. How does it happen (or not happen)?

MOSES

Called, but Frustrated

The character who figures most prominently in the entire Old Testament, the leader who is either the most successful or the most frustrated ever, is Moses. He was Israel's leader at its originative moment, at its most decisive turning point, not because he rose up through the ranks or was lifted up as the most brilliant or charismatic by his people. He had gotten in trouble, fled the country, and was nestled securely in the middle of nowhere, watching over his father-in-law's sheep, when God called him to do this miraculous, yet exasperating leading.

Moses was a shepherd. We may harbor notions of shepherds as humble, lowly, poorly paid laborers. But in the Ancient Near East, flocks could number in the tens of thousands, requiring considerable administrative savvy. So we should not be surprised that the Sumerians, Akkadians, Assyrians, Babylonians, Egyptians, and Greeks spoke of their greatest leaders as "shepherds" of the people. Picturing better rulers in the future, God promised the Israelites, "I will give you shepherds after my own heart" (Jer 3:15). Christians have been devoted to Jesus as "the good shepherd." Tim Laniak wrote that

> God's chosen leader Moses was trained for his role as shepherd of flocks in the deserts of Sinai.... Israel's ideal king, David, is similarly called from tending flocks to become the shepherd of God's people.... They

are themselves extensions of the divine Shepherd who leads the covenant community by his hands.[1]

Without overly romanticizing the vision of the shepherd's role, we can mull over the way shepherds were responsible to care for the sheep: ensuring adequate food and water, leading them to pasture, making space for rest, providing security, and fending off menacing threats.

How is leading today like shepherding? Pope Francis reflected on bishops who "supervise/oversee" versus those who "keep watch," like a shepherd:

Overseeing refers more to a concern for doctrine and habits, whereas *keeping watch* is more about making sure that there be salt and light in people's hearts....To *watch over* it is enough to be awake, sharp, quick. To *keep watch* you need also to be meek, patient, and constant in proven charity. *Overseeing* and *watching over* suggest a certain degree of control. *Keeping watch*, on the other hand, suggests hope, the hope of the merciful Father who keeps watch over the processes in the hearts of his children.[2]

Career and Calling

Professionally, Moses was a shepherd. But God called him to very different work or perhaps to a very different kind of shepherding, the way Jesus called fishermen to become fishers of people. Moses's call story is mind-boggling, but typical. Minding his own business (literally), Moses was drawn to an unusual sight and voice. When God calls, is it because God places something so dramatic in front of us (in this case, a bush that burns but doesn't) we can't avert our gaze? Or is there some unsatisfied yearning, a hollow place, an attentiveness even to human suffering that draws us toward God's mind and heart?

God laid out what needed to be done. Like all of us, Moses explained why he couldn't do it. *I don't know your name. They won't follow me. I have severely curtailed speaking abilities.* As Robert McAfee Brown put it, "Moses ducks and weaves in every possible way to avoid the body blow of the assignment."[3] But God persisted and reassured. It seems that weakness only eggs God on. Inability, even disability, does not frighten God. This God looks for availability.

Jeremiah's objection was that he was too young. Reasonable—and there are always those who will dismiss the leadership we need. *She's too young and inexperienced. He's "unrealistic"*—that chiding adjective that proves the one doing the labeling is hopelessly jaded and cynical. The world needs the young, with their bold naïveté, to speak out. Jonah's reply to God was to hightail it down to Joppa and jump on board a ship headed to Tarshish—the opposite direction and as far away as possible from Nineveh. Who doesn't shudder over the times we've plunged headlong away from God's summons? In the Bible, Isaiah was the only one who was actually praying when God called. This God invades our space, so it is where you live and work that God is likely to speak.

"Calling" isn't confined to the clergy. God calls all people to big and little things, to do this for a living, to do that this afternoon. God asks us to do hard things or the simplest, easiest things. The question isn't *What do I want to do?* or *What do I want to do for God?* but *What does God want me to do?*

Examples of people fulfilling their divine vocation are all around us. In my most formative years, I watched my grandfather answer God's calling every day as a rural mail carrier. He was unfailingly kind, delivered medicine to shut-ins, stopped to pray with the elderly or lonely, and was a wise fixture in his small town of Oakboro, North Carolina, all his adult life.

God's calling may begin in a sensitive soul that is troubled by the news. While most people hear of the troubles of the world and shudder, fume, or change the channel, some are drawn in. Their hearts are "broken by the things that break the heart of God," as Bob Pierce, the founder of World Vision, used to say.[4] And they can't do nothing. Soon they are out crusading, writing letters, organizing volunteers, or even finding a low-paying career in rabble-rousing or alleviating suffering.

Others see human suffering and try their hand at politics or medicine or law. Playing a part in God's project of bringing healing and wholeness to the world, in some small way, is the fulfillment of the call. Then perhaps just saying a prayer, writing a note, or giving up your seat on the bus to someone who's struggling is the fulfillment.

Leaders can be attentive to and responsive to God's calling in what priorities are established, in how others are treated, in policies and pricing. Sometimes a leader will hear God's call to exit the place and do something else perhaps lower on the food chain. Sometimes a leader is asked by God to stay in a tough, unrewarding situation to be a little candle in an otherwise dark place.

Women Leading in Moses's Story

In the background of Moses's story are four striking women. Jochebed, his mother, about whom we know precious little, must have been remarkable, brave, and resourceful. Her three children, Moses, Aaron, and Miriam, became great leaders.

Then we see Shiphrah and Puah, the midwives who defied, with sassy impertinence, the pharaoh's orders to kill every male infant. When asked why they refused his command, they said, "Because the Hebrew women are not like the Egyptian women; for they are vigorous and give birth before the midwife comes to them" (Exod 1:19). Like Rosa Parks and so many other women without official titles through history, they led an underground movement of civil disobedience. Biblical leadership so often takes just this form: defiance by seemingly insignificant people with no power at all against the world's powerful leaders and their laws. As Sacks points out, "There are crimes against humanity that cannot be excused by the claim that 'I was only obeying orders.'"[5] There are always leaders, even those vested with the power to punish, who should not be followed.

Jochebed defied the pharaoh in her own way by hiding her son. But this gambit could not last long. In desperation, or in faithful hope (and we may ask how different these really are), she placed her three-month-old son in a basket and set it afloat on the Nile River. The Hebrew word for this basket, *tevah*, occurs only one other time in scripture: to describe Noah's ark. Both ark and basket were rudder-less, lacking locomotion, carrying the future hope of humanity toward who knows where. This *tevah* floated right up to the spot where Pharaoh's daughter happened to be bathing. Nothing is explicit, but we sense God somehow brought basket and princess together. Leaders should recall various chance circumstances and twists in the plots of their lives that led them to some place, to somebody, and be a little awestruck by the hidden goodness that they can't be sure was God, but then they would bet it probably was.

A weak, vulnerable child in the corridors of the mighty: Moses wound up being raised in the household of Pharaoh himself, whose vaunted reign he was destined to subvert. Moses was parented and educated, not with the rest of the Hebrews chafing under slavery but in the royal household, where he was afforded a superb education and an insider's awareness of what went on in the corridors of power, which served him well years later when he returned to that very palace to take on those powers. At what age did he realize he wasn't really an Egyptian? How does great leadership unfold when you finally discover your solidarity with the oppressed, with the seemingly lowly?

Pharaoh's moodiness tells us something about power, authority, and leadership. Historians argue over which pharaoh was on the throne when the Israelites took off. If it was in fact Rameses II, then the story of God's rescue operation is even more spectacular, as Rameses II was the greatest of all the pharaohs. Yet our story portrays him as riddled with anxiety. He dreaded what might happen if Israel's population grew. He treated them with increasing ruthlessness, demanding ever more production and then foolishly (and to us, hilariously) taking away straw from the brickmakers. His paranoia had already driven him to kill off the males—his labor supply. This pharaoh's crazed decision-making feels exaggerated, but we can all think of leaders whose anxiety and paranoia drive institutions and people down into a dark hole. The lust to cling to power bedevils leadership.

Stand Still and See Deliverance

Moses arrived on the scene and immediately met with the elders of the Israelites. Somehow, they bought in, believing against all reasonable hope that deliverance was forthcoming. Why didn't they just laugh their heads off? They sensed God heard their cries and cared simply because Moses showed up. It's fascinating how just showing up, how simple listening, earns much leadership capital.

At the outset, Moses claimed his own weakness. Among several objections he raised when called by God at the burning bush was his speech defect. Did he actually stammer? Or was he simply "not eloquent"? The Hebrew word *kabad* means "heavy." His tongue was heavy? Would anyone have the oral savvy to talk down Pharaoh? Medieval rabbis taught that this failure in Moses's speech was symptomatic of a larger "exile of the word."[6] When people are in bondage, language itself is alienated and repressed, words lose their meaning, truth is elusive. Clearly, anyone who would lead today must speak in a world where words and truth don't seem to count for much.

Not surprisingly then, Moses's attempts to lead failed repeatedly. In his first appearance in Pharaoh's court he was humiliated. The plagues he unleashed only drew the ire of his own people as their lot only worsened. Once Moses finally got them to the sea's edge, when they heard the rumbling of Pharaoh's chariots in pursuit, the people wailed in horror, pleading with him to take them back. His response was not to turn and fight or flee in a zigzag escape route. Instead, with Pharaoh's juggernaut bearing down on them, he said to the people, "Stand firm, and see the deliverance that the LORD will accomplish for you today" (Exod 14:13). Do...nothing at all.

Perhaps Jehoshaphat thought of this moment centuries later when he said, "We do not know what to do, but our eyes are on you" (2 Chr 20:12). Perhaps the psalmist had been so spiritually intoxicated by this moment that he quite effortlessly wrote on God's behalf, "Be still, and know that I am God" (Ps 46:10). No secular leadership manual will ever counsel doing nothing or simply looking to God for a miracle. But the theologically attuned leader will come upon quite a few brick walls where a calm, holy, seemingly weak, do-nothing approach will be the only thing to do—and the best thing to do.

Who was the first to step into the water? According to the rabbis it was Nahshon, son of Aminadav. Only after Nahshon actually waded into the water did the sea part so everyone else could cross over. That first person to step forward is always the key. Retelling this story, Elie Wiesel imagined the people panicking, dashing headlong away from the pharaoh in terror. Moses raised his hand and ordered a halt: "Wait a moment. Think, take a moment to reassess what it is you are doing. Enter the sea not as frightened fugitives but as free men!"[7]

To witness a walk to freedom is liberating. Nelson Mandela walked out of a prison in South Africa into the history books. John Lewis, who became a congressman from Georgia, pointed to a photograph of himself as a young seminarian being released from prison in Nashville. His face glowed with a dignity and confidence: "I had never had that much dignity before. It was exhilarating—it was something I had earned, the sense of the independence that comes to a free person."[8]

In the Wilderness

One would imagine that after such a blockbuster event, Moses's place as leader would have been unquestioned and secure. But perhaps in the way Winston Churchill was summarily dumped as prime minister as soon as the war that would never have been won without him had ended or in the way pastors who guide a church through an arduous building campaign often lose their support once the people get into their new digs, Moses enjoyed no carryover. Having escaped vile servitude, the people whined incessantly and treated Moses shabbily. Clergy often joke that in every church there is a "back to Egypt!" committee.

> The whole congregation of Israelites complained against Moses and Aaron.... "If only we had died by the hand of the LORD in the land of Egypt, when we sat by the fleshpots and ate our fill of bread; for you have brought us out into this wilderness to kill [us] with hunger." (Exod 16:2-3)

God responded by giving them bread. No one thanked Moses. No sooner had they eaten than the people "quarreled with Moses," castigating him for lack of water. God told Moses to strike the rock, and water gushed forth. Still the people never fell in love with Moses.

Jonathan Sacks reads a lot into Moses's subsequent career, and in thoughtful ways. When Moses raised his hands against the Amalekites he grew weary; his sagging arms were then held up by Aaron and Hur (Exod 17:12). He wasn't performing some miracle with his raised hands; he was inspiring and reminding his people that they could succeed. Sacks declares, "A leader must empower the team. He cannot do the work for them; they must do it for themselves. But he must, at the same time, give them the absolute confidence that they can do it and succeed."[9] That ragtag band of Israelites would have been surprised by the idea that they were an empowered team.

Moses had to learn he couldn't bear the leadership burden alone. His father-in-law, Jethro, took pity on him, offering wise counsel to engage in what today we call "delegation" and "role clarification."

> What you are doing is not good. You will surely wear yourself out, both you and these people with you. For the task is too heavy for you; you cannot do it alone.... You should represent the people before God, and... teach them.... You should also look for able men among all the people, men who fear God, are trustworthy, and hate dishonest gain; set such men over them as officers.... It will be easier for you, and they will bear the burden with you. (Exod 18:17-22)

The burden they all came to share was Moses's greatest gift to them: his delivery of the Torah, the law, hundreds of laws, life-giving command-ments designed not to afflict or imprison the people but to set them free, to live into God's holy mercy. Can you feel the delight in Zora Neale Hurston's retelling of the moment holiness came down the mountain?

> Moses lifted the freshly chiseled tablets of stone in his hands and gazed down the mountain to where Israel waited. He knew a great exultation. Now men could be free. They had something of the essence of divinity expressed. They had the chart and compass of behavior. They need not stumble into blind ways and injure themselves. This was bigger than Israel. It comprehended the world. Israel could be a heaven for all men forever, by these sacred stones. With flakes of light still clinging to his face, Moses turned to where Joshua waited for him. "Joshua, I have laws. Israel is going to know peace and justice."[10]

How do leaders help others to understand the way rules and struc-tures aren't crushing but liberating? And are the rules and structures in place actually so?

Renewal, and How to Lead God

In those wilderness years, the real leading of the people was done by the Lord, who used a cloud of glory by day and a pillar of fire by night. Moses had to have lived in a constant state of exasperation, for Martin Buber was right: "Whenever he comes to deal with this people, he is de-feated by them."[11] Exodus 32 provides the most dramatic example of his failed leadership, but in that moment Moses discovered a renewed calling.

Moses was far away on top of the mountain for longer than the peo-ple had anticipated. So they concluded that Moses was delaying (why?), and began to refer to him as "this Moses," not "our beloved Moses." So they fashioned an idol, a golden bull, the kind they'd seen back in Egypt, connoting strength, potency, virility. At that very moment, God was telling Moses what their gold was supposed to be used for: to adorn the tabernacle.

The Lord saw their lunacy first and told Moses, speaking of them not as "my people" but "your people" whom "you" (Moses, not I, the Lord!) brought out of Egypt. Moses turned the tables just as swiftly, referring to them not as "my people" but as "your people whom you" (the Lord!) brought out of Egypt. Down in the valley, Aaron his brother had proven to be an effective but wrongly directed leader. Once the calf was finished, they threw a big party. When Moses happened upon the scene, Aaron violated Jim Collins's rule for Level 5 leaders (leaders attribute success to others and apportion blame to themselves[12]) and explained how "they" were set on evil. He bore no responsibility. Hilariously he recalled what transpired: "I said to them, 'Whoever has gold, take it off'; so they gave it to me, and I threw it into the fire, and out came this calf!" (Exod 32:24).

What Moses achieved in this moment astonishes us. God was determined to pour wrath down on the people and be done with them. But Moses argued with God, marshaling his case that God should relent: "Turn from your fierce wrath; change your mind" (v. 12). And Exodus 32:14 reports that "the LORD changed his mind." Moses led God! Oddly enough, as Michael Walzer observes, Moses was "rather more successful with God than with the people."[13] Moses, struggling to lead the people for decades, had pretty fair results in leading God, pleading successfully on behalf of his people.

This intercessory role is an intriguing aspect of leadership. Pastors pray for parishioners with various illnesses, but do pastors intercede with God, asking for mercy on the people for their waywardness? Frustrated leaders in business can always mope, vent, or sign up for the latest leadership seminar, but do they get on their knees and plead with God on behalf of their coworkers? In families, do we ask for God's healing mercy on one another?

The Freedom of Letting Go

Moses, for all of his sorrows and frustrations, still stands for us as the greatest of all leaders. Fittingly, "Moses was very humble, more so than anyone else on...earth" (Num 12:3). His greatness was that "the LORD knew [him] face to face" (Deut 34:10). This intimacy with God issued in signs and wonders, none as amazing as these words he spoke to his people: "You shall not abhor any of the Edomites, for they are your kin. You shall not abhor any of the Egyptians, because you were an alien residing in their land" (Deut 23:7). In other words, no hating, even if you have been hated. The Edomites were distant kin (through Jacob and Esau), but the relationship had been riddled with tension for centuries. Moses reminded them and us that blood kinship is as broad as all of humanity.

Who could tolerate—much less love—the Egyptians, those cruel oppressors? Jonathan Sacks put it beautifully:

> If the people had continued to hate their erstwhile oppressors, Moses would have taken the Israelites out of Egypt but would have failed to take Egypt out of the Israelites. They would still be slaves, not physically but psychologically. They would be slaves to the past, held captive by the chains of resentment, unable to build the future. To be free, you have to let go of hate.[14]

Indeed, Moses achieved the highest conceivable level of leadership. He made people better than they might have dreamed of being. He showed them the way to kindness and nobility—how to be like God. Moses knew the way because he had immersed himself thoroughly, humbly, and without reservation in the mind and heart of God.

In the end, we come to the tragedy that takes your breath away. Jim Collins shows how it is essential for great leaders to pursue a BHAG, a "big, hairy, audacious goal."[15] Moses's would be hard to top. He hauled a nation right to the brink of the promised land, his life's project finally in sight, and then he was denied entry. We can point to that bizarre moment when Moses evidently didn't strike the rock in the right way, and God retaliated: "Because you did not trust in me, to show my holiness before the eyes of the Israelites, therefore you shall not bring this assembly into the land that I have given them" (Num 20:12). But is God that petty? Didn't Moses out-sanctify everyone else by far? Moses himself blamed the people (Deut 3:26). Maybe Franz Kafka was right:

"Moses fails to enter Canaan, not because his life is too short, but because it is a human life."[16] After decades of arduous labor, having finally gotten a glimpse of the broad expanse of the land from his viewpoint atop Mount Nebo, Moses died. He wasn't there to see or enjoy the fruit of his life's work.

Isn't this always the way? We are all part of something bigger than ourselves. The best leading we do happens after we are gone. Our successors continue and expand the life of a church or a business or a family after we've departed. Who can picture Moses's final day without recalling Martin Luther King Jr.'s final hours? In Memphis, campaigning on behalf of garbage workers, he spoke eerily of his possible impending death: "I've been to the mountaintop. . . . I've seen the promised land. I may not get there with you. But. . . we as a people will get to the promised land."[17]

We might also ponder Reinhold Niebuhr's pithy wisdom:

> Nothing that is worth doing can be achieved in our lifetime; therefore we must be saved by hope. Nothing which is true or beautiful or good makes complete sense in any immediate context of history; therefore we must be saved by faith. Nothing we do, however virtuous, can be accomplished alone; therefore we are saved by love.[18]

Israel's loss was immense, but God provided a new leader, as always. Perhaps there would never be another Moses. But there was a Joshua.

Study Questions

1. How might leading be more like shepherding, like watching over the flock?

2. What breaks God's heart?

3. Do you think of what you do as a calling, or a career? And what difference does it make?

4. When have you seen the need for defiance?

5. How can rules and structures be liberating instead of suffocating?

6. How do you feel about this picture of Moses leading God?

7. What was something you labored long and hard for, but you didn't get to enjoy the completion?

8. What do you think about Niebuhr's idea that nothing worth doing can be achieved in your lifetime?

JOSHUA AND SAMSON

Commitment and Burnout

The books of Joshua and Judges narrate the hazy, complicated, and occasionally embarrassing history of Moses's successors. Joshua is often remembered for his blitzkrieg triumph over the Canaanites. But his greatest moment as leader came not long before his own death. With all the tribes gathered at Shechem, he rehearsed Israel's sacred story, fixing their attention on what today we might call "institutional memory," eliciting gratitude, awe, and a sense of a far larger purpose than they'd thought about earlier that morning. Then he named what would be the main thing after his departure—not securing the next great leader, but a choice they had to make: to revere and serve the Lord or revert to the foreign gods of old.

Then, instead of threatening or even pleading, he made personal witness: "As for me and my household, we will serve the LORD" (Josh 24:15). In countless situations, our only recourse is to speak in the first person and simply declare, as Martin Luther did centuries later, "Here I stand." To be sure they wouldn't renege or drift, he wrote down his and their commitment and erected a big rock under an oak tree as a witness to the moment. Printed, visible words for businesses, churches, and families to rally around and a focal emblem everyone sees and values: leaders know people need these things.

The saga of Israel's legendary leaders in the closing days of the Bronze Age is earthy, and not terribly inspiring. There was no institution to lead. God spontaneously inspired temporary leaders when various crises required it. Ehud stabbed Eglon of Moab, who was so fat the sword was swallowed up by his belly. Deborah defied stereotypes as she sat under a palm tree dispensing judgment and leading Israel in battle against Sisera, who was dispatched by Jael, who drove a tent peg into his temple with a hammer. Jephthah, son of a prostitute, struck a foolish bargain with God by vowing to slaughter the first person who came out to meet him if only God helped him defeat the Ammonites. Who greeted him? His daughter, his only child. The book of Judges careens downhill from there.

Squandered Giftedness

A telling study in leadership can be made of the life of Samson. Swashbuckling, reckless, muscular, capable of prodigious feats, extraordinarily gifted. But then he stumbled; he squandered his gifts. His failure? He tiptoed down what *Hamlet* called the "primrose path of dalliance," as so many leaders do.[1] Some are caught. Others get away with it. All are weakened by it, along with everyone around them.

Samson dallied with alcohol and sex. His drunken affair was with Delilah (whose name means "flirtatious"), who was bent on taking advantage of him. The irony is that Samson was on to her. He knew what she was up to. Three times, he evaded her trap. But finally he caved in, and told her his secret: "A razor has never come upon my head.... If my head were shaved, then my strength would leave me" (Judg 16:17).

But why? He just got worn down. She nagged; she pestered him to death. He simply burned out. This phenomenon of burnout has been analyzed and dealt with in many books, workshops, personnel manuals, and counseling sessions. It is real, and the biblical prescription for burnout is fairly simple. You have limitations. You need rest, or Sabbath, which is a different sort of rest from weekends or vacations. Sabbath is time with God, time for God, putting all our other times into perspective. You were made for the freedom and energy of holiness, but you are a broken, vulnerable person, in constant danger of stumbling, and thus in need of much help. You can live into a deep sense of purpose, and belonging, because of your place in God's community, buoyed by the love of God and the people of God.

As a young man, Martin Luther King Jr. preached a sermon that addressed the avoidance of temptation, the renewal of calling, and the beauty that leadership can be. It was Christmas 1951. King climbed into his father's pulpit in Atlanta; sitting in the congregation was a young soprano, Coretta Scott, whom he had brought home to meet his parents. The sermon, "How the Christian Overcomes Evil," was punctuated with an analogy from mythology. The sirens sang their haunting, seductive songs, luring sailors and their ships onto the rocks and shipwreck. Ulysses managed to get through by stuffing wax into ears of his sailors and strapping himself to the mast of the ship. Strong stuff. But King said the Christian way to overcome evil was exemplified not by Ulysses but by Orpheus. When approaching the sirens and their songs, Orpheus simply pulled out his lyre and played an even more beautiful song, so the sailors were allured by his music and did not even hear the sirens.[2]

Study Questions

1. How does one know when to take a firm stand and invite others to follow?

2. When have you seen extraordinary giftedness squandered?

3. Have you experienced burnout?

4. How can a person be restored after squandering giftedness or burning out?

PRIESTS

Thinking and Acting Institutionally

One of the remarkable relics in the Israel Museum in Jerusalem is a stone altar from Arad, a town southeast of Jerusalem, found in 1962 by the archaeologist Yohanan Aharoni. A temple dedicated to the worship of Israel's God was built there around the days of Elijah—or so we think. Traces of the last burnt incense offered to God were scattered across the top of the limestone. It was a stunning archaeological find.

When I look at that altar, I wonder who the priest was who administered that last burnt offering. Someone knew how to handle this altar, what to do, how to invite worshippers into the presence of God while ensuring proper reverence, awe, and dignity. People didn't randomly stroll up and sacrifice any old way they wished. There were specialists, the priests of ancient Israel, well-trained, the trustees of sacred space. Holiness—God's, and thus the people's—was their business.

The Virtue of Anonymity

The priests were the generally nameless leaders from Old Testament times with whom the people had the most regular contact. Sadly, if we know their names it is because they misbehaved or abused their office. Hophni and Phinehas, Eli's sons, "were scoundrels; they had no regard for the Lord or for the duties of the priests to the people" (1 Sam 2:12-13). They gobbled up sacrifices for themselves; they rudely ignored Eli's correction. Like neighborhood bullies, they were too strong for the job.

Unlike other leadership positions, being a priest was never about personal gain, fame, glory, or advancement. One might aspire to be high priest, who got that rare glimpse inside the Holy of Holies. But even most of the high priests' names have been lost to history. There was a desired anonymity; it was all about the office and never personality. Individual achievement would not be possible. The priests were without credentials or resumes. They weren't even "called." Priesthood was the family business. Yes, there was training, but you became one by being born.

So while in our society we think of leadership as creative, dynamic, charismatic, and individualistic, with the Israelite priesthood we see a very different kind of leadership: anonymous, utterly uncreative, unassertive, playing a crucial role in the lives of the people by leading them to God, but never pioneering bold new strategies or striding out where no one had gone before. Lots of leadership in our world is just as rote and anonymous.

Priestly leadership was conservative by design. Greg Jones coined the term *traditioned innovation* to describe the leadership churches require nowadays:

> Traditioned innovation is a way of thinking and living that holds the past and future together in creative tension, a habit of being that depends on wise judgment, requiring both a deep fidelity to the patterns of the past that have borne us to the present and a radical openness to the changes that will carry us forward. Our feet are firmly on the ground with our hands open to the future.[1]

The priest would nod at the word *traditioned* and shrink back at the word *innovation*. The priest was most himself when he did what had always been done. This maintaining of order is crucial even today when whatever is newfangled gets the hype and good press. Church leaders who are entrepreneurial are praised, but the priest who stands at the altar and recites the Eucharistic prayer, just as he has every day for his forty-year career and just as the priest before him did, leads in the most profound way imaginable.

The priests are exemplars of a kind of leadership that is underrated today. Hugh Heclo has written marvelously of what he calls *thinking institutionally*—that despite our culture's anti-institutional mood, we function well and even thrive when we live into the truth that we who lead are part of institutions larger than ourselves.

> Institutional thinking understands itself to be in a position primarily of receiving rather than of inventing or creating. The emphasis is not on thinking up things for yourself, but on thoughtfully taking delivery of and using what has been handed down to you.[2]

We all are "debtors who owe something, not creditors to whom something is owed."[3] Heclo adds, "Having a realistic, sober view of our human condition, the institutionalist understands that people usually have a greater need to be reminded than to be liberated."[4] Institutional reminding might not sound glamorous, but isn't it essential?

And what's really going on? Think about it: we view routine and repetition as dull and mundane. Details are for subordinates, nonleaders. But with the priesthood, it was the routine that ushered the worshipper out of the mundane and into the heavenly. Priests in Israel did what clergy do today: they make what is miraculous routine and accessible, or perhaps they make what is routine and accessible the stuff of miracle. Amos Wilder was thinking of Old Testament-like worship when he provocatively suggested that

> going to church is like approaching an open volcano, where the world is molten and hearts are sifted. The altar is like a rail that spatters sparks, the sanctuary like the chamber next to an atomic oven; there are invisible rays, and you leave your watch outside.[5]

Mind you, the lava, sparks, and rays really are dangerous. While today we have lost the sense of God's numinous holiness before which you rightly tremble, in Israel people approached the holy God with caution and trepidation. And they needed assistance, as Richard Nelson explains,

"Priests insulated worshippers from direct contact with the hazards of sacred space and holy things, yet priests also provided the connections that brought divinity near and made life with Yahweh possible."[6]

The Grace of Daily Obligation

It is the routine that has proven trustworthy over time as the way to God's heart. Perhaps in the way we need personal trainers or yoga instructors, we need leaders who can guide us toward good habits and steady discipline in fitness, health, the workplace, and certainly the life of faith. Annie Dillard was visiting a church on Puget Sound when the priest, kneeling at the altar leading the prayers, stopped suddenly, looked up to the ceiling, and cried out, "Lord, we say these same prayers every week!" Then the service proceeded. Dillard wrote, "Because of this, I like him very much."[7] We grow as people of faith when we discover the truth and glory in Kathleen Norris's lovely phrase "repetition as a saving grace."[8] Whatever we repeat is who we are; the repetition of all the little acts of worship, prayer, gathering, offering, and song will prove to be our saving grace.

The humble, nameless leaders who are office-holders, the steady as you go solid rock at work, those uncreative readers of our holy books may play the steady, reliable role we need when the charismatic leaders are out there doing who knows what. Consider Gail Godwin's marvelous assessment of Father Gower:

> He's not trendy; he doesn't pose. He's neither a self-transcendent guru nor one of these fund-raising manager types who have become so sought after lately by our Holy Church. He's just himself—himself offered daily. He worries about people, he worries about himself....He goes to the hospital carrying the Sacraments in his little black case. He baptizes and marries and buries and listens to people's fears and confessions and isn't above sharing some of his own. He scrubs the corner cross with Ajax....He makes his services beautiful; he reminds you that the whole purpose of the liturgy is to put you in touch with the great rhythms of life. He's a dedicated man, your father. He's lonely

and bedeviled like the rest of us, but he has time for it all and tries to do it right. He lives by the grace of daily obligation. He's what the priests in books used to be like, but today he's a rarity.[9]

Priests in Old Testament times offered themselves daily, and their services were beautiful.

And we can be sure they worried about people. Only an insensitive dolt could have watched the same sorrowful woman bringing her modest sacrifices, weeping in the sanctuary, and not felt her pain. There was a pastoral tenderness in the implementation of ritual as we see in the story of Hannah. Barren and taunted by her husband's other wife, Hannah prayed repeatedly and with such intensity that Eli surmised she must be drunk. After she explained her plight, he engaged in his regular priestly function by offering her a word of blessing: "Go in peace; the God of Israel grant the petition you have made to him" (1 Sam 1:17).

This notion that words of blessing conveyed divine grace and power is alien to us. But each one of us can recall moments when words were spoken and the world changed. *It's malignant. I love you. I'm proud of you. I forgive you.* In Israel the priests were mouthpieces of God and spokesmen for the people to God. The oldest scraps of Bible archaeologists have ever found are two little scrolls of thinly hammered out silver, with Numbers 6:24-26 scratched onto the surface: "The Lord bless you and keep you; / the Lord make his face to shine upon you, and be gracious to you; / the Lord lift up his countenance upon you, and give you peace." The larger one is a mere three and a half inches by one inch! And both of them, found on the outskirts of ancient Jerusalem, are dated to the eighth or seventh century BCE (making them nearly three thousand years old!).[10] Leaders understand the power of and the need for spoken words of blessing.

The priests invoked the divine mystery and blessed people who were in dire need of some mercy. All leadership requires compassion and discernment. The laws were clear, but priests were constantly confronted with he said, she said scenarios. *He killed my sheep. I did not; your sheep fell off the cliff.* Or *He slept with my wife. I did not.* And while we cannot know the emotional dynamics of confession and atonement, there must have been priests who were told *I have sinned*, and then proceeded to shame the sinner. And there must have been other priests who acknowledged the grievousness of sin but cared and kindled hope for healing.

In all these priestly responsibilities, ordering the worship of the people, administering justice, handling sacrifices, ensuring the proper care for the temple precincts, and rendering faithful judgments of law, attention to detail was essential. In every profession, there are aspects of the work that are all about detail, the proper ordering of things, ensuring that the bedrock of tradition holds. There is a powerful symbolism in minute detail. Danny Meyer is notorious for stopping at any table in any of his restaurants and moving the saltshaker however slightly if it's not in the center. He believes this kind of "constant, gentle pressure," and attention to a seemingly minor detail, creates an atmosphere of excellence everywhere.[11]

There can be a steady delight for the leader and for those being led when order is restored. Leadership in detail and even leadership in holiness are so needed today. Nelson's description of the priest's responsibility is intriguing: "The priest lived out the holiness that was required of the whole people"; he "bore their sins," and "his righteousness brought joy."[12]

Gratitude as Love in Action

As we contemplate priestly leadership, it is important to weigh the significance of what over time became their principal specialty: the administration of sacrifice. We miss the deep meaning of sacrifice if we think of it as mere expungement of guilt, of placating an angry God. Mind you, guilt mattered in Israel. Whatever was impure had to be dealt with, and seriously. And God wasn't a warm, fuzzy, indulgent deity but a holy, jealous God. The miracle is that this holy, jealous God sought an intimate relationship with each person, as Nelson clarifies: "The truly distinctive factor in Israel's understanding of sacrifice was Israel's God,

Yahweh."[13] Israel's worshippers felt they were "interacting with the personal and gracious God."[14]

The word *sacrifice* is itself intriguing: it means to "make holy." So to think of myself as someone who sacrifices: it's not putting on a long face and grudgingly giving up something I prefer to keep. I make what I have holy. By what I sacrifice to God, I discover the way to make all that I have holy. In Israel, a worshipper brought a sheep to sacrifice, partly to consecrate the rest of the sheep left in the pen. How do we make whatever we have at home or in the world holy? And who leads in that peculiar endeavor?

The real heart of sacrifice is twofold: the expression of gratitude and the healing of fractured relationships. In Israel, when the wheat finally ripened, instead of rushing in to bake the loaf for which your family was desperately hungry, you took that first grain and burned it on a stone altar, the smoke curling heavenward as an expression of thanks to the one who sent the rain and made the soil yield something good. If your flock of sheep prospered, you expressed gratitude by killing and burning the most stalwart male (not the runt), the one any rational person would assume you needed for next year's breeding. Yet if you trusted God, this was the sheep that you gave up, proving you knew the sheep and your future belonged to God in the first place.

In Israel, gratitude, and the declaration of who was God and who wasn't, was entirely tangible and costly. Perhaps this could be a transformative lesson for us. As Mother Teresa said,

> You must give what will cost you something. This is giving not just what you can live without, but what you can't live without or don't want to live without. Something you really like. Then your gift becomes a sacrifice which will have value before God. This giving until it hurts, this sacrifice is what I call love in action.[15]

In church life, and in all of life, this kind of sacrifice matters. The leader sets the example. And the humility of the practice of gratitude is the key to all leadership. God made us for gratitude; leaders express gratitude relentlessly.

Even secular researchers can demonstrate the benefits of gratitude. Psychiatrist Martin Seligman explains some simple exercises that research has proven will significantly lift your sense of well-being. Instead of focusing on what goes wrong and how to fix it, we zero in on what goes well. His formula? "Every night for the next week, set aside just ten minutes before you go to sleep. Write down three things that went well today, and why they went well. Use a journal, or your computer—as it is important to have a physical record."[16]

Seligman asked depressed women and men to do this. After a week, their depression scores lowered by half, and their happiness scores doubled. His studies show similar results for people who take up the habit of expressing gratitude in writing to others. For two thousand years, Christianity has recommended prayers of gratitude and thanksgiving at the end of each day. Saints have kept lovely journals full of the kind of thing Seligman commends. Church life, corporate life, family life—all flourish when gratitude is the order of the day. Those who express thanks lead best.

Healing What Is Broken

And then there were the sacrifices that were intended to repair what had been fractured. Through Leviticus we read what was to be done when neighbors conflicted, when the community broke down, when sin intruded. A precious animal was cut up on the altar so that the blood could run down. This bloodshed may seem ghastly. What did God have in mind, asking for this pouring out of blood? Is God a sadistic despot? The Bible, if you read the whole thing, portrays a God who is humble and compassionate, placing immense value on the life God created.

Somehow the sacrificing of precious animals was something of a lesson in living. Israelites were taught to value life so much that, if you know it will cost you your best ram or goat, you'd think twice before hurting your neighbor. Here's how it worked: ancient people believed the healing power of God was hidden in the blood. Today we know what they knew: when relationships are broken, no matter how hard we try, we can never fully repair the damage. Some residue of guilt lingers. My soul, our marriage, a fractured community—the mythical bleeding never quite stops. The Old Testament understood and believed that only God's power, God's healing energy, released by the sacrifice of something precious, could bridge that gap and finish the healing.[17]

The leadership the priest provided, finding the way to reconciliation among those with broken relationships, is essential in all leadership, although the corporate world does not own the language of forgiveness and reconciliation. But this is the challenge of leadership: how to bring wholeness and healing where lives and relationships are brittle and broken, how to relieve guilt, how forgiveness can and must happen.

The priests were also teachers. God told Aaron, and thus all his descendants, the priests, "You are to distinguish between the holy and the common, and between the unclean and the clean; and you are to teach the people . . . all the statutes that the LORD has spoken to them through Moses" (Lev 10:10-11). Great teachers dazzle the mind with subtle distinctions, and students learn how to distinguish between passable but lazy thought and excellent, more truthful thought. Leaders teach. Attention to detail and subtle distinctions matter. In this pivotal role as the teachers of God's law to the people, the priests shared responsibility with the sages, to whom we now turn.

Study Questions

1. How do you feel about this idea of anonymous leadership?

2. Why does our society value creativity and personality more than tradition and office?

3. How does leadership happen in mundane details?

4. Have you experienced this "grace of daily obligation"?

5. Why is attention to detail so important?

6. Gratitude matters. When have you been thanked (or not), and how did it make you feel?

7. Could forgiveness and reconciliation find a firmer footing where you live and work?

SAGES

Elusive Wisdom

Finally, after forty years of wandering in the wilderness, the Israelites arrived at the brink of the promised land. On the high ridge of Mount Pisgah, looking out over the Jordan River valley into the promised land, God instructed Moses to "choose for each of your tribes individuals who are wise, discerning, and reputable to be your leaders" (Deut 1:13).

I had the good fortune to learn about the sages of Israel from a teacher who was himself quite the sage: Father Roland Murphy, a Roman Catholic Old Testament scholar of impeccable virtue and sparkling personality. He was brilliant, having published hundreds of items and was fluent in a dozen languages. Many recall him as the greatest teacher ever. At his memorial service, I reminded everyone of the way he would hold the Bible and read some especially sumptuous passage. Before commenting, he would scrunch up his face and emit a guttural sound reminiscent of a bear chomping down on a hunk of meat. He loved scripture. He loved the church. He loved God.

And he loved me. That love manifested itself in that virtue about which he was a world-renowned expert: wisdom. He didn't know *about* wisdom. He *was* wise. I learned at his feet, by his side, in his company. I never made an important decision without consulting with him.

Beyond Conventional Wisdom

Business consultants are aware of the importance of "emotional intelligence,"[1] self-awareness, self-regulation, empathy, and social skill—all akin to wisdom. Does wisdom "work"? Maybe, and maybe not—but we know how desperately we need a steady source of wisdom. Leadership that is wise may succeed, but it is always fruitful. Every organization needs that peculiar leadership, maybe from the boss but maybe not, that we would call wise.

Wisdom is elusive nowadays. We know smart people and successful people. But who is wise? Wisdom can be had by someone with a low IQ or someone who lives out in the middle of nowhere. Brainpower might actually crowd out wisdom. Ralph Waldo Emerson praised Harvard for having "all the branches of knowledge," only to have Henry David Thoreau retort, "Yes, but none of the roots."[2] Wisdom is deep underground, not just lying around on the surface. Wisdom ponders the end and the purpose of life. Wisdom steps outside the moment and perceives broader and more personal implications. Wisdom is perspective. Wisdom is patient, centered, not easily thrown off balance. Wisdom takes time, and must be cultivated. Wisdom usually is born out of the cauldron of experience. You can't just pick up a notion and become wise the way you crack open a fortune cookie. You live it, wait on it, test it, let it seep into the good earth through the soles of your feet.

In Israel, in little villages and even in the big city, there were sages. There may have been schools where wisdom was taught, but those would have been reserved for the elite. In most places, the wise lived down the road. They often sat in the city gate to adjudicate controversies; people sought them out there and asked questions. These elders earned their reputation, as Aaron Chalmers explains: "These are the people that an 'average Israelite' would have sought out.... This group gained their authority from the confidence placed in them by the townspeople who recognized their wealth of experience and hence wisdom."[3] Most were men, but many were women (2 Sam 14, 20).

The ideal was that there would be a couple of sages in every home: mom and dad were responsible for the sharing of wisdom. Much of the Bible's wisdom reflects this intimate bond: "Hear, my child, your father's instruction, / and do not reject your mother's teaching" (Prov 1:8). But by extension, the wise man who sat in the city gate, unrelated by blood, still used such language when speaking tenderly to whomever came for advice: "My child, if sinners entice you, / do not consent" (v. 10). I never called Father Murphy "Dr. Murphy" or "Roland," although he would not have minded. He was, in the style of biblical wisdom, a father to me; I longed to be a good son to him. Institutions need father and mother figures.

Israel's sages would occasionally craft an extended speech. But generally they preferred short, gnomic, memorable sayings. Our book of Proverbs is a collection of some of their most unforgettable sayings.

> Whoever winks the eye causes trouble. (10:10)
>
> Fools think their own way is right, / but the wise listen to advice. (12:15)
>
> When the ways of people please the LORD, / he causes even their enemies to be at peace with them. (16:7)
>
> The beginning of strife is like letting out water; / so stop before the quarrel breaks out. (17:14)
>
> The words of a whisperer are like delicious morsels; / they go down into the inner parts of the body. (18:8)
>
> If you close your ear to the cry of the poor, / you will cry out and not be heard. (21:13)

Each one of these invites some reflection and even conversation.

Contrast biblical wisdom with the silly soundbytes that pass as "conventional wisdom" today:

> Time is money.
>
> You get what you pay for.

When the going gets tough, the tough get going.

Do unto others before they do unto you.

Life is short, play hard.

Bloom where you are planted.

Behind every man there's a good woman.

Beggars can't be choosers.

It's hard to soar like an eagle when you work with turkeys.

People will repeat these like mantras and nod as if they are onto something deep. But triviality isn't wisdom; mirroring values that aren't of God fosters a corporate climate that alienates us from God and others. Christian leaders at home, work, and church shoulder the responsibility to show us a better, deeper way.

Emotional Maturity

Rabbi (and family therapist) Edwin Friedman, in his marvelous, thoughtful book on leadership, *A Failure of Nerve*, clarifies that leading is not about techniques and strategies or even hard work. In our overly reactive society, we look for quick-fix saviors and forget to look for leaders who might calm our anxiety. We need leaders who are "emotionally mature" and wise. "Children rarely succeed in rising above the maturity level of their parents, and this principle applies to all mentoring, healing, or administrative relationships."[4] The leader, like the sages of old, recognizes emotional forces in play in a given company and society at large. Friedman suggests we look for "the well-differentiated leader"— one who can "focus first on their own integrity and on the nature of their own presence rather than through techniques for manipulating or motivating others."[5] This maturity only dawns when the leader has worked through issues from his or her family of origin. Failure doesn't stem from lack of effort or insufficient data, or even a bad choice of strategy.

So Friedman is all about a new kind of self in the leader, an inner strength that is hardly dependent on technique, information, or even the particular challenges of the company being led. Jim Collins (in *Good to Great*) suggests that corporate vitality does not hinge on the charisma and personal greatness of the leader; in fact, he and others suspect that the strong personality might prove to be counterproductive.[6] Friedman could not disagree more. He certainly would eschew a sick personality that only appears to be 'big' on the outside. But the healthiest, strongest personality possible is the leader's best gift to the organization. "The expression of self in a leader is what makes the evolution of a community possible."[7] Institutional problems

> are not the result of an overly strong self in the leader, but of a weak or no self. Democratic institutions have far more to fear from lack of self in their leaders and the license this gives to factionalism (which is not the same as dissent) than from too much strength in the executive power.[8]

Could it be that the best route to faithful leadership might be time spent in slow, contemplative reading of the literature Israel's sages have bequeathed to us? Perhaps leaders should get outside more and invite others to do the same. "Go to the ant, you lazybones; / consider its ways, and be wise" (Prov 6:6). The wonder of wisdom in the Bible is that so often there is no "point" or "lesson." We simply learn to ponder, to be in awe, and the soul grows. Consider this:

> Three things are too wonderful for me;
> four I do not understand:
> the way of an eagle in the sky,
> the way of a snake on a rock,
> the way of a ship on the high seas,
> and the way of a man with a [woman]. (Prov 30:18-19)

All you can do is sigh, and pause in gratitude for the mystery and sheer wonder of being. This is wisdom. This is the stuff of leadership.

The wisdom traditions of scripture exhibit a robust, positive view of human nature. The title of Walter Brueggemann's early book on wisdom, *In Man We Trust*, underscores an under-noticed aspect of who we are as God's people. Yes, we are broken, mortal sinners. But we are fashioned in God's image. God has given us minds, hearts, and a surprisingly large capacity for wisdom. We can trust others, including leaders, even in this age of suspicion. We can trust ourselves. We had better learn to trust ourselves because God most clearly trusts us. God has placed the future of God's endeavors in our hands. Yes, God helps; God sometimes overrules; God keeps a close hand on things. But we are the priesthood of believers, ushering one another toward God. We are the prophets to hear and implement God's words of challenge and hope. We are leaders who can lead in holy ways. We are God's sages.

Our Common Humanity

And yet to speak in this way does not imply any narrowness, as if we who read these scriptures have a corner on wisdom. Far from it. From the very beginning, there was something international, even interfaith about biblical wisdom. From all over the ancient world we have wisdom from Babylon, Greece, Ugarit, with thousands of parallels to the Bible's wisdom. Along trade routes, among diplomats, and when merchants sipped wine over late-night dinners, wisdom was shared, translated into various tongues, adopted by diverse religions. Truth was welcomed wherever it could be found. Marriage, parenting, business, aging, death, and friendship frustrate, delight, and humble everyone with a pulse.

In our divided world where whoever is different is demonized, wisdom builds a bridge. The wise find ways to listen, to understand; we embrace new perspectives, which do not threaten but enrich what we think we already know. Leadership hinges on the deft handling of differences—a happy openness to divergent viewpoints and beliefs, helping everyone to find good in any and every place.

The ultimate common denominator in our shared life is suffering. We need wise leadership the most—in church, at work, at home—when we try to cope with darkness. Wisdom in Israel did not avert its gaze from suffering. The book of Ecclesiastes is an extended meditation on the hollowness of life. Blunt in its cynicism, Ecclesiastes stares the potential pointlessness of life in the face. And no one rushes in late in the book to say something sunny about God or resurrection or healing. Real life isn't like that anyhow. There is a sorrow, an emptiness at the core of life in the world and in each person's gut. There is meaningless suffering. No wonder chaplains during the Vietnam War reported that Ecclesiastes was the book soldiers most often requested to be read aloud.

The book of Job isn't a theological treatise on why bad things happen to good people. But we do get an intense, up-close look at a righteous man who suffers unspeakably. No glib explanations or justifications will do. Job's so-called friends tried just that. With little tact or compassion, Eliphaz reminded Job that God is fair: God rewards the righteous. Perhaps Job hadn't been as upright as he'd imagined. Besides, God was probably teaching Job a lesson. Bildad suggested that if Job would just pray, God would come down and make everything better. Zophar, the deep thinker, proclaimed that we cannot understand God's will; we must merely accept it.

Job was not comforted. In fact, their words offended. "You whitewash with lies; / ...you are worthless physicians" (Job 13:4). They spouted theology, but their shrewd thinking about God only isolated Job sadistically from God. His gut screamed out that he had been dealt a terribly unfair hand. Their ridiculously simple answers only falsified the more mysterious truth of God by pasting trite religiosity on top of his grief that was beyond all answering. Lest we think Job should have been less touchy and simply thanked them for their pious greeting cards, God himself thundered against Job's friends at the end of the story: "You have not spoken of me what is right" (42:7).

How often do we find ourselves groping for meaningful words to salve the wound of a coworker, friend, or family member? Are there some Bible verses I can send? Shuddering over his friends' well-intended counsel, Job cried out, "If you would only keep silent, / that would be your wisdom!" (13:5). Notice he didn't say "Go away." Just be here, and show up; there is no need for words. We have this terrible craving to fix things, to produce a smile and make it all okay. But no fancy theological footwork can remedy the ache. The mystery of grace is not captured in syrupy little sound bites. God's love is manifest in our tears when we simply sit in the darkness.

Every leader confronts sorrow, tragedy, sudden death, horrific loss. The accountant's wife is diagnosed with ovarian cancer. The custodian's husband is killed in an accident. There are layoffs to be announced. The marketing guy is going in for substance abuse treatment. The guy who was the life of every staff party takes his own life. Grandma had a heart attack. Leadership can come from all over when the news comes. Often it's the quiet, unassuming type who stands like a rock and simply weeps. Or it's the chatterbox who holds up a hand and says *Let's be silent for a while*. The leader, the one who is usually the leader, is wise to cultivate healthy feelings and responses in the face of suffering. These moments stamp the organization for good or ill for years to come.

Study Questions

1. Whom do you know that is wise? What wisdom have you garnered from them?

2. Where do you hear conventional wisdom, and why is the superficial so appealing to people?

3. How can wisdom be cultivated?

4. Do you think Collins or Friedman is right about the importance of a strong personality in a leader?

5. How is wisdom related to the passing of time and the ability to be awestruck?

6. When have you seen suffering or a tragedy handled well or poorly?

PETER AND PAUL

Downward Mobility

The story of the birth, survival, and growth of the early church is nothing short of miraculous. Jesus's first followers were untrained and frankly too chicken to stick it out to the crucifixion. If we try to piece together what the "structure" or "strategy" of the early church looked like, we wind up confused or chuckling. Tensions couldn't be resolved, nobody had a plan, and then there was sporadic persecution. Even the theology they were stuck with was an embarrassment. Graffiti has been found mocking Christianity, one with a donkey impaled on a cross. Larry Hurtado has quite rightly asked a tough question: in light of the economic distress and social ostracisim Christians bore, *Why on earth did anyone become a Christian in the first three centuries?*[1] His book bearing that title gives a few answers, and none of them have anything to do with strength, impressiveness, or brilliance. The two primary leaders who made it happen, or with whom it happened, were Peter and Paul.

It's fair to say Jesus never spoke stranger words than "You are Peter, and on this rock I will build my church" (Matt 16:18). Peter was a rock in the way sandstone qualifies as a rock. In that very moment, Peter chided Jesus for even thinking about getting himself crucified. Peter was brave enough to make it to the courtyard, but then denied even having met Jesus (Matt 26:70). Not the stuff of great leadership. "Fishing" was his resume.

122

Peter had his strengths surely. But when it came to leading a worldwide religious movement, Peter had nothing to offer. What he had, as it turned out, was enough. He inspected the empty tomb, and was "amazed" (Luke 24:12). Later he saw the risen Lord—and then, when he spotted him cooking breakfast, Peter jumped into the sea and swam ashore only to be quizzed by Jesus: "Simon son of John, do you love me more than these?" Dizzied by the encounter, and taken aback by the questions, Peter struggled to explain his love for Jesus, who then asked him to lead: "Feed my lambs" (John 21:15).

If we read on, we discover something crucial about biblical leadership. Peter was weak but determined, passionate but inept. But no matter: Jesus had chosen him. And the form his leading would take illustrates the portrait of a leader we've seen through all of scripture. Jesus mysteriously told him, "When you were younger, you used to fasten your own belt and go wherever you wished. But when you grow old, you will stretch out your hands, and someone else will fasten a belt around you and take you where you do not wish to go" (John 21:18). John darkly alluded to Peter's untimely death. What kind of leading is martyrdom?

The Way of Vulnerability

Henri Nouwen's *In the Name of Jesus*, one of the very best books on leadership, is a profound meditation on this moment. He names the perilous temptations of leadership so common in our culture but toxic in Jesus's community. In the face of the urge to be "relevant," the follower of Jesus, like Peter by the lakeshore, "is called to be completely irrelevant and to stand in this world with nothing to offer but his or her own vulnerable self. That is the way Jesus came to reveal God's love."[2] For him the question isn't "How much are you going to accomplish?" but "Are you in love with Jesus?"—which is what Jesus asked Peter. The skill set then is a willingness to pray, to be struck by the beauty of the Lord, and to want nothing but to listen to him and be close to him.

The second temptation is to be popular, or spectacular, but all Peter is asked to do is to feed sheep—and not his sheep but Jesus's sheep. Then third, leaders are tempted to be powerful, to exercise control. As Nouwen points out, one of the ironies of history is that Christian leaders have forgotten how Jesus resisted the devil's wiles, and they have instead seized power, rationalizing that by ruling or warring or wielding authority they were doing a good thing for God. The leading Jesus asked of Peter was not to assume authority but to be bound, to be led, to be weak.

> The way of the Christian leader is not the way of upward mobility in which our world has invested so much, but the way of downward mobility ending on the cross. . . . I am speaking of a leadership in which power is constantly abandoned in favor of love.[3]

We know little about Peter's eventual leadership. He had to have been as surprised as anybody by the response to his preaching for which he had no training and which wasn't much more than a series of Bible verses strung together. The book of Acts portrays him with a newfound boldness: healing a lame man, and getting himself arrested and coping with abuse. Two things had changed in Peter. The Holy Spirit had rushed on him, with the others, and he had received mercy from the risen Lord. Weakness co-opted and put into holy service: this is how leadership happens.

Years later, in Joppa at the home of Simon the Tanner, Peter "fell into a trance. He saw . . . something like a large sheet coming down" (Acts 10:10-11). Filled as it was with animals deemed unclean by Jewish law, Peter was repulsed. But a voice told him to eat—and not just the food. He was to eat with Cornelius, a centurion, the kind of Roman official Peter had loathed all his life. Peter's weakness was the kind of prejudice that is reality-based, entirely understandable, and even justified by scripture.

Poor Peter. His spine was never very strong. Earlier he had tried eating with Gentiles, but shrunk back when James's people showed up (Gal 2:11). The one who denied Christ three times still was capable of waffling. But he was the one God chose, and used. How often does Christian leadership, in church life or out in the world, involve a daring crossing of social boundaries? How much of leadership is simply being the one to sit down with the stranger, the one the righteous have judged? And then isn't leadership the awareness that criticism is coming and to deal with it as humbly and creatively as the very action that elicited the criticism in the first place?

And to linger on the clash between Peter and Paul in Antioch, we may ponder the virtue of ugliness in meetings. Jean Vanier reminds us to be calm and hopeful: "Leaders should not be surprised if meetings sometimes bring explosions. If people express themselves violently, this is because of an anguish which we should respect."[4] Indeed, from a biblical perspective, the leader understands someone may have felt wronged or that someone may be on the verge of growth or that everyone goes through a tough day. We can provide a haven, a space for compassion.

Paul, Servant Leader

Finally we come to the fitting ending to our study of biblical leadership. The Apostle Paul traveled more than ten thousand miles as he organized and solidified a worldwide church—partly by dint of will, but primarily by something simpler: thinking deeply and clearly. Paul wrote Christian theology when there was none at all. Leadership must provide a vision, clarity of thought, and sometimes it has to be invented on the fly yet still be compelling and enduring. N. T. Wright explains Paul's leadership by the pen:

> He wrote energetic and powerful Greek....He was capable of powerful and lyrical passages which show a poetic touch and an almost Beethoven-like ability to move from thunder and lightning to soft moonlight and back again. His style is his person, his tongue like a bell flinging out broad his name....He was doing theology because the life of God's people depended on it.[5]

In Paul's timely, multifaceted letters we find two types of material in which he reflects on leadership. The first is precisely what most people would be looking for in a book about biblical leadership. In 1 and

2 Timothy, we find Paul outlining a recipe of the character and habits of the faithful Christian leader:

> A bishop must be above reproach, married only once, temperate...an apt teacher, not a drunkard, not violent but gentle, not quarrelsome....keeping his children submissive....Deacons likewise must be serious...not indulging in much wine. (1 Tim 3:2-8)

By these standards, wouldn't David be ousted, Abraham deemed unqualified, Esther not even under consideration?

But did Paul actually write these letters? Even if he did, doesn't his counsel feel a bit simplistic, aloof, unrealistic, and even downright dull after the complex story lines full of struggle, dysfunction, confusion, surprise, luck, and sheer mercy and providence we've explored in the stories of Saul, David, Elijah, Esther, and Moses? It's almost as if the author didn't know the stories of the Bible's greatest leaders, or the author thought it wise to head off the problems they suffered—as if such a thing is possible for real, broken, fallen human beings.

What is far more intriguing about Paul, regarding leadership, is the way he seems almost reluctant to speak of leadership at all, reminding us of Jonathan Goldingay's comment that in the Old Testament the very idea of *leadership* is a problem, nothing but a concession to human sinfulness, and thus those who lead only manage to sin more spectacularly than everyone else.[6] The Greek language featured many words for leadership, but Paul only used a couple, and sparingly. He was fond of speaking of the Christian life and its leadership as *diakonos*, service/servant; then he was downright prolific in his use of the word *doulos*, slave, to describe himself. Who was weaker in the caste system of the Roman empire than servants and slaves?

Power Perfected in Weakness

How obsessed was Paul with the reality of the crucified Jesus when he spoke of the church, not as a company or government with budgets and strategies but as Jesus's Body? And how glued was Paul to Jesus and his deep care for the weakest when he declared that the most important member of the Body, and hence the one entrusted with leadership, was the weakest member of that Body (1 Cor 12:22-25)? Paul's leadership workshop has two agenda items: Jesus, and people who are lowly.

Paul never shied away from talking about *power*. But for him, power was a problem; the powers were insidious manifestations of evil, dressed up impressively but spelling doom for God's people. The powers existed, not to be seized by the Christians but to be crushed by the Lord. "Our struggle is…against the cosmic powers of this present darkness" (Eph 6:12). "He disarmed the rulers and authorities and made a public example of them, triumphing over them" (Col 2:15).

The most dramatic, subversive, and compelling theme in Paul's talk about leadership is the way he countered his critics by speaking of his failures. Instead of hiding his weaknesses, or compensating for them, he blurts out in the open his maladies and inadequacies, as if they are trophies. Accepting the charge that he was neither trained nor skillful in speech—reminding us of Moses!—Paul bragged that "I came to you in weakness and in fear and in much trembling" (1 Cor 2:3)—reminding us of Jehoshaphat. "We have become a spectacle. . . . We are fools for the sake of Christ. . . . We are weak" (4:9-10).

Andrew Clarke, a scholar on the topic of Paul's theology of leadership, suggests that "it is likely that Paul is here speaking with more than a hint of irony."[7] But Paul isn't being clever; this isn't self-effacing manipulation. He *was* weak and relished being weak—because of his intimate relationship with the crucified Jesus, who became weak. The gospel is not about a powerful God or a God who masquerades briefly as weak only to leap out from behind the curtains to show how mighty he really is. All measures of power are inverted, and shattered, by the humble, holy, compassionate, merciful, and thus weak heart of God. Struggling to express himself, Paul was compelled to use the word *power*, but it simply doesn't mean power any longer.

> The message [of] the cross is foolishness to those who are perishing, but to us who are being saved it is the power of God. . . . God's foolishness is

wiser than human wisdom, and God's weakness is stronger than human strength....God chose what is weak in the world to shame the strong; God chose what is low and despised...to reduce to nothing the things that are. (1 Cor 1:18, 25, 27-28)

Our best theologians have fixated on this, not as yet one more truth about God but as the deepest truth in the very heart of God. Bonhoeffer understood that "the Bible directs man to God's powerlessness"[8]—for only such a God can help. Jürgen Moltmann explained why weakness is better than omnipotence: "A God who is only omnipotent is in himself an incomplete being, for he cannot experience helplessness and power-lessness. Omnipotence can indeed be longed for...but omnipotence is never loved; it is only feared."[9] This God would be loved, and lovers never coerce; they only wait in their weakness, longing in hope.

Paul had his unseemly moments, when he was fully capable of putting down his foes with strident sarcasm. But even that failure was embraced as yet another weakness that kept him close to the heart of Jesus. When his leadership was hotly contested, he ultimately responded, not by flexing his muscle or thrashing his foes but by the most startling confession imaginable. "If I must boast, I will boast of the things that show my weakness" (2 Cor 11:30). Indeed, he reports that the Lord spoke to him, saying "My grace is sufficient for you, for power is made perfect in weakness" (12:9).

The noblest, holiest Christian leadership happens where there is weakness, humility, anonymity, struggle, and failure. Michael Knowles, in his powerful book on Paul's weakness in preaching, wrote these words of encouragement for all leaders who question whether they matter:

> The vast majority of preachers throughout the entire history of the Christian church have conducted their ministries in either relative or absolute obscurity. And they, by virtue of such obscurity, best exemplify cruciform preaching as Paul intends it. Wherever preachers stand before their congregations conscious of the folly of the Christian message, the weakness of their efforts, and the apparent impossibility of the entire exercise...there, Paul's homiletic of cross and resurrection is at work. The one resource that genuinely faithful preachers of the gospel have in abundance is a parade of daily reminders as to their own

inadequacy, unworthiness and—dare we admit it—lack of faithfulness. Yet these are the preconditions for grace, the foundations for preaching that relies on God "who raises the dead."[10]

Are you weak enough to lead? Do you know the grace in the cross and resurrection?

Study Questions

1. How do you feel about the fact that Christianity thrived in a hostile environment without a clever business plan or trained leaders?

2. What if you offered (as Nouwen suggested) nothing but your vulnerable self? And that the ideal is downward mobility?

3. Can you recall a meeting where there was ugliness? Was there some good that came of it?

4. How do you feel about Paul's strategy of responding to his critics by revealing his weaknesses?

5. What do you think about these ideas about God not being omnipotent but vulnerable and powerless?

6. Have you ever experienced strength being perfected in weakness?

7. Are you weak enough to lead?

EPILOGUE

How Weakness Helps

Near the beginning of this book, when we pondered the weakness of Jesus on the cross, we recalled Dietrich Bonhoeffer's puzzling, powerful words: "God lets himself be pushed out of the world on to the cross. He is weak and powerless in the world, and that is precisely the way, the only way, in which he is with us and helps us."[1] How can weakness help?

In his marvelous book on Jesus's path from strength and control to weakness and suffering, *The Stature of Waiting*, W. H. Vanstone notes how in any setting,

> nothing so disrupts the normal and expected procedure of a meeting as the physical collapse of someone who is present....The presence of a helpless person suddenly generates in such a situation a whole new range of possibilities....As a result of his helplessness, a great many things happen which would not otherwise happen.... The helpless person becomes, in his helplessness, extremely important.[2]

To imagine such a scene might clear our vision a bit when we think about leadership. Yes, skills, smarts, training, savvy, and experience matter. We are constantly pelted with pressure to enhance all of these. So how curious is this? Jesus, Paul, Jeremiah, Elijah, Saul, David, and the others we've spent time with in this book appear somewhat uninterested in the usual prescriptions for how to lead well. But they do seem to be obsessed in varying ways with God and that elusive, mysterious, and yet healing intersection between their own weakness and God's mercy, patience, and providence. Each one of them, in one form or another, collapsed helplessly.

Because they did, a great many things happened, and we're still talking about them. They are, in their brokenness, God's word and palpable presence to us. Their leadership may even be subtly distinguished from the ideal popularized by Robert Greenleaf: *Servant Leadership*.[3] The servant leader's primary desire is to serve, most often from a position of strength. This is good, of course. But Hudson Taylor, a pioneer English missionary to China, was onto something better: "God chose me because I was weak enough. God does not do his great works by large committees. He trains somebody to be quiet enough, and little enough, and then he uses *him*."[4]

The liberation in learning you are weak enough to lead is twofold. First, it is always theologically truer to say *I am weak and broken* than *I am strong and capable*. This isn't self-recrimination, wallowing in self-pity, or clinging to negative messages absorbed in childhood. It is the joyful clarity that humility brings and the holy bonds we discover with others. We need not wait for the physical collapse of someone before noble things happen. We are all broken already. Let the outpouring of mercy begin.

And second, when we lead out of our weakness, we are very close to Jesus, who was handed over, silent before his accusers, meek before his attackers, and inert as he was laid in the tomb. Jesus led with nothing but love. When Jesus led in weakness, he was not pretending, as if playing out some divine charade. What we see in Jesus is who God truly is. I'm fond of what may be the better translation of Philippians 2:6: instead of "Although he was in the form of God he emptied himself," we should read "Because he was in the form of God he emptied himself."[5] Indeed. It was precisely because he fully was God and transparently unveiled the heart of God that Jesus came as a humble nobody and consorted with nobodies and laid down his life, bearing shame and abandoning all privilege. Michael Gorman called the cross "the signature of the Eternal

One."[6] The Christian leader—while properly interested in things running smoothly, staff relationships, and bottom lines—is above all else obsessed with Jesus and wants not just to please or follow him but to be like him and to be one with him.

So leaders embrace their inevitable weakness, their created limitations, and are unafraid to share and live out of that weakness. Should a leader then just bleed all over the floor? Not really. Sometimes out of love you just have to keep it to yourself—and you always do whatever you do for the sake of others, as Andy Crouch explains:

> The leader's own personal exposure to risk must often remain unspoken, unseen and indeed unimagined by others.... The leader must bear the shared vulnerabilities that the community does not currently have the authority to address.... When leaders take risks, including the risks of personal disclosure, they do so for the sake of others' authority and proper vulnerability.[7]

Now that's leadership: leading in the sharing of vulnerabilities.

No physical collapse disrupts the normal functioning of a room the way simple aging does. The Bible teaches us "to count our days" (Ps 90:12), to measure life as a gift, and yet one with mercifully prescribed limits. We are all getting weaker and closer to our end all the time. Perhaps there is no greater weakness than dementia. Memory, the repository for joys for which to be grateful and wounds that need to be healed, is our great treasure, and to lose it is immense sorrow. The lone yet glorious hope for those who cannot remember is that they are not forgotten by God. God has tethered God's own self to the promise of redemption—of all that has been, of whatever has been forgotten, and also the might-have-beens and should-have-beens.

What will God remember about the leading I have done? This question isn't a threat but a plaintive invitation to me to do whatever I do now for the only one who will remember it all. It won't be numbers or profits or popularity or effectiveness that will matter in eternity. It will be that "while we were still weak, Christ died for [us]" (Rom 5:6). So let us be weak enough. It shouldn't be hard at all, because we already are.

NOTES

Epigraph

J. C. Pollock. *Hudson Taylor and Maria: Pioneers in China* (Grand Rapids: Zondervan, 1967), 125; cited in Michael P. Knowles, *We Preach Not Ourselves: Paul on Proclamation* (Grand Rapids: Brazos, 2008), 54.

Stanley Hauerwas and Jean Vanier, *Living Gently in a Violent World: The Prophetic Witness of Weakness* (Downers Grove, IL: IVP, 2008), 34–35.

Introduction

1. Jonathan Sacks, *Lessons in Leadership: A Weekly Reading of the Jewish Bible* (New Milford, CT: Maggid Books, 2015), xxi.

2. Ibid.

3. John Goldingay, *Old Testament Theology: Israel's Life,* vol. 3 (Downers Grove, IL: IVP Academic, 2009), 708–11.

4. Ibid.

5. Bill George, Peter Sims, Andrew N. McLean, Diana Mayer, "Discovering Your Authentic Leadership," *Harvard Business Review* 85, no. 2 (February 2007): 129–38.

6. Ibid.

7. Ronald A. Heifetz, *Leadership Without Easy Answers* (Cambridge, MA: Belknap, 1994), 2.

8. Elaine A. Heath, *The Mystic Way of Evangelism: A Contemplative Vision for Christian Outreach* (Grand Rapids: Baker Academic, 2008), 12.

9. Edwin H. Friedman, *Generation to Generation: Family Process in Church and Synagogue* (New York: Guilford, 1985), 208.

10. Karl Barth, *The Word of God and the Word of Man*, trans. Douglas Horton (New York: Harper and Row, 1957), 186.

11. Brené Brown, *Daring Greatly: How the Courage to Be Vulnerable Transforms the Way We Live, Love, Parent, and Lead* (New York: Avery, 2012); Patrick Lencioni, *The Advantage: Why Organizational Health Trumps Everything Else in Business* (San Francisco: Jossey-Bass, 2012), 27–37.

Jesus

1. Hans Urs von Balthasar, *Unless You Become Like This Child*, trans. Erasmo Leiva-Merikakis (San Francisco: Ignatius, 1991), 49.

2. Roland Bainton, *Here I Stand: A Life of Martin Luther* (New York: Signet, 1950), 236.

3. Danny Meyer, *Setting the Table: The Transforming Power of Hospitality in Business* (New York: HarperCollins, 2006), 233.

4. Amy-Jill Levine, *Short Stories by Jesus: The Enigmatic Parables of a Controversial Rabbi* (New York: HarperOne, 2014), 199.

5. Frye Gaillard, *If I Were a Carpenter: Twenty Years of Habitat for Humanity* (Winston-Salem, NC: John F. Blair, 1996), 13.

6. Anna B. Warner, "Jesus Loves Me," *The United Methodist Hymnal* (Nashville: The United Methodist Publishing House, 1989), 191.

7. Hans Urs von Balthasar, *Mysterium Paschale: The Mystery of Easter*, trans. Aidan Nichols (San Francisco: Ignatius, 1990), 118, 115.

8. Dietrich Bonhoeffer, *Letters and Papers from Prison*, ed. Eberhard Bethge (New York: Macmillan, 1971), 360.

Hannah

1. Wendell Berry, *Hannah Coulter* (Berkeley, CA: Counterpoint, 2004), 113.

2. Maggie Ross, *The Fountain & the Furnace: The Way of Tears and Fire* (New York: Paulist, 1987), 80.

Saul

1. My paraphrase.

2. Timothy S. Laniak, *Shepherds After My Own Heart: Pastoral Traditions and Leadership in the Bible* (Downers Grove, IL: Intervarsity, 2006), 97. Emphasis in original.

3. Ronald A. Heifetz and Marty Linsky, *Leadership on the Line: Staying Alive Through the Dangers of Leading* (Boston: Harvard Business School), 2002.

4. David M. Gunn, *The Fate of King Saul: An Interpretation of a Biblical Story* (Sheffield, England: JSOT, 1980), 65, 115, 125.

5. Nassir Ghaemi, *A First-Rate Madness: Uncovering the Links Between Leadership and Mental Illness* (New York: Penguin), 2011.

6. Eugene F. Rogers Jr., *After the Spirit: A Constructive Pneumatology from Resources Outside the Modern West* (Grand Rapids: Eerdmans, 2005), 189.

7. Heath, *The Mystic Way of Evangelism*, 12.

David

1. Francesca Aran Murphy, *1 Samuel* (Grand Rapids: Brazos, 2010), 167.

2. J. R. R. Tolkien, *The Lord of the Rings: The Fellowship of the Ring* (New York: Ballantine, 1955), 298.

3. Gerhard von Rad, *The Problem of the Hexateuch and Other Essays*, trans. E. W. Trueman Dicken (London: SCM, 1984), 201.

4. Murphy, *1 Samuel*, 175.

5. Malcolm Gladwell, *David and Goliath: Underdogs, Misfits, and the Art of Battling Giants* (New York: Little, Brown and Co., 2013).

6. Jeffrey A. Krames, *Inside Drucker's Brain* (New York: Portfolio, 2008), 68–81.

7. Lewis A. Parks and Bruce C. Birch, *Ducking Spears, Dancing Madly: A Biblical Model of Church Leadership* (Nashville: Abingdon, 2004), 71.

8. Walter Brueggemann, *First and Second Samuel* (Louisville: John Knox, 1990), 174.

9. Lovett H. Weems, *Church Leadership* (Nashville: Abingdon, 2010), 98.

10. Meyer, *Setting the Table*, 90.

11. Krames, *Inside Drucker's Brain*, 131.

12. Hauerwas and Vanier, *Living Gently in a Violent World*, 64.

13. This "representative" understanding was beautifully articulated in an unpublished article by Thomas A. Langford entitled "The Character of Ordination."

14. Patrick Lencioni, *The Advantage: Why Organizational Health Trumps Everything Else in Business* (San Francisco: Jossey-Bass, 2012), 1.

15. Patrick Lencioni, *The Five Dysfunctions of a Team: A Leadership Fable* (San Francisco: Jossey-Bass, 2002).

16. Laniak, *Shepherds After My Own Heart*, 104.

17. David Wolpe, *David: The Divided Heart* (New Haven, CT: Yale University Press, 2013), xiv.

18. Ibid., 20.

19. Jim Collins, *Good to Great: Why Some Companies Make the Leap . . . and Others Don't* (New York: HarperBusiness, 2001), 50.

20. Robert Barron, *2 Samuel* (Grand Rapids: Brazos, 2015), 62.

21. Peter Scazzero, *The Emotionally Healthy Leader* (Grand Rapids: Zondervan, 2015), 72–80.

22. Wolpe, *David*, 96.

23. Barron, *2 Samuel*, 161.

Kings and a Queen

1. Jean Vanier, *Community and Growth* (New York: Paulist, 1989), 216.

2. Heifetz, *Leadership Without Easy Answers*, 184. I owe this line of thought on Esther to my doctoral student Jennifer Strickland, who wrote an outstanding paper on the subject.

3. Ibid., 201, 204.

4. David J. A. Clines, *The Esther Scroll: The Story of the Story* (Sheffield, England: JSOT, 1984), 153.

5. Ibid., 156–57.

Elijah

1. Ronald A. Heifetz and Donald L. Laurie, "The Work of Leadership," *Harvard Business Review*, 1997; reprinted in *On Leadership* (Boston: Harvard Business Review, 2011), 61.

2. John Goldingay, *Old Testament Theology: Israel's Life*, vol. 3 (Downers Grove, IL: IVP Academic, 2009), 777.

3. Walter Brueggemann, *Truth Speaks to Power: The Countercultural Nature of Power* (Louisville: Westminster John Knox, 2013), 86–87.

4. Derek Sivers, "How to Start a Movement," *TED*, video, 3:09, from TED2010 in February 2010, http://www.ted.com/talks/derek_sivers_how_to_start_a_movement?language=en#t-129681.

5. Rowan Williams, *Being Christian: Baptism, Bible, Eucharist, Prayer* (Grand Rapids: Eerdmans, 2013), 27.

6. Jonathan Sacks, "Elijah and the Still, Small Voice (Pinchas 5775)," *Rabbi Sacks*, July 6, 2015, http://rabbisacks.org/elijah-and-the-still-small-voice -pinchas-covenant-conversation-5775-on-ethics/.

7. Mother Teresa, *A Simple Path* (New York: Ballantine, 1995), 7.

Elisha

1. Sacks, *Lessons in Leadership*, xxvii.

2. See our new collection of wise essays: eds. Craig T. Kocher, Jason Byassee, and James C. Howell, *Mentoring for Ministry: The Grace of Growing Pastors* (Eugene, OR: Cascade, 2017).

3. Tolkien, *The Lord of the Rings: The Fellowship of the Ring,* 302.

4. William Manchester, *The Last Lion: Winston Spencer Churchill, Visions of Glory 1874–1932* (New York: Dell, 1983), 34.

5. Collins, *Good to Great,* 36.

6. Thomas Merton, *New Seeds of Contemplation* (New York: New Directions, 1961), 189.

Micaiah

1. Harry G. Frankfurt, *On Bullshit* (Princeton, NJ: Princeton University Press, 2005).

2. Chris Lowney, *Heroic Leadership* (Chicago: Loyola Press, 2003), 29.

3. Lencioni, *The Advantage,* 27.

4. Anne Lamott, *Bird by Bird: Some Instructions on Writing and Life* (New York: Anchor, 1994), 87.

5. Peter J. Leithart, *1 & 2 Kings* (Grand Rapids: Brazos, 2006), 161.

6. Ibid.

Jeremiah

1. Goldingay, *Old Testament Theology,* 3:783.

2. Jack R. Lundbom, *Jeremiah Among the Prophets* (Eugene, OR: Cascade, 2012), 57.

3. Peter Scazzero, *Emotionally Healthy Spirituality: It's Impossible to Be Spiritually Mature While Remaining Emotionally Immature* (Grand Rapids: Zondervan, 2006). See also, *The Emotionally Healthy Leader: How Transforming Your Inner Life Will Deeply Transform Your Church, Team, and the World* (Grand Rapids: Zondervan, 2015); and *The Emotionally Healthy Church: A Strategy for Discipleship That Actually Changes Lives* (Grand Rapids: Zondervan, 2015).

4. Vanier, *Community and Growth,* 47.

Amos, Second Isaiah

1. Goldingay, *Old Testament Theology*, 3:783.

2. Warren G. Bennis and Robert J. Thomas, "Crucibles of Leadership," *Harvard Business Review* 80, no. 9 (September 2002), 39–45.

3. John Goldingay, *The Theology of the Book of Isaiah* (Downers Grove, IL: IVP Academic, 2014), 71.

4. Henri Nouwen, *The Wounded Healer: Ministry in Contemporary Society* (New York: Doubleday, 1972).

Genesis

1. Sacks, *Lessons in Leadership*, 4.

2. Ibid., 8.

3. Ibid., 11.

4. Ibid., 38–39.

5. Daniel Burnham, quoted in Charles Moore, *Daniel H. Burnham, Architect, Planner of Cities*, vol. 2 (Boston: Houghton Mifflin, 2012), 147.

6. Heifetz and Laurie, "The Work of Leadership," 60.

7. Claus Westermann, *Genesis 37–50: A Commentary*, trans. John J. Scullion (Minneapolis: Augsburg, 1986), 205.

Moses

1. Laniak, *Shepherds After My Own Heart*, 75.

2. Austen Ivereigh, *The Great Reformer: Francis and the Making of a Radical Pope* (New York: Picador, 2014), 263–64. Emphasis in original.

3. Robert McAfee Brown. *Unexpected News: Reading the Bible with Third World Eyes* (Philadelphia: Westminster, 1984), 38.

4. Richard Stearns, *The Hole in Our Gospel* (Nashville: Thomas Nelson, 2009), 9.

5. Sacks, *Lessons in Leadership*, 63.

6. Avivah Gottlieb Zornberg, *Moses: A Human Life* (New Haven, CT: Yale University Press, 2016), 11–12.

7. Elie Wiesel, *Messengers of God: Biblical Portraits and Legends* (New York: Summit, 1976), 193.

8. David Halberstam, *The Children* (New York: Fawcett Books, 1998), 140.

9. Sacks, *Lessons in Leadership*, 80.

10. Zora Neale Hurston, *Moses, Man of the Mountain* (New York: Harper Perennial, 1991), 233.

11. Martin Buber, "Biblical Leadership," *On the Bible: Eighteen Studies*, ed. Nahum Glatzer (Syracuse: Syracuse University, 2000), 142.

12. Collins, *Good to Great*, 36.

13. Michael Walzer, *Exodus and Revolution* (New York: Basic Books, 1985), 67.

14. Sacks, *Lessons in Leadership*, 271.

15. Collins, *Good to Great*, 237.

16. Franz Kafka, *The Diaries of Franz Kafka, 1910–1923*, trans. Martin Greenberg and Hannah Arendt (New York: Schocken, 1988), 394. Quoted in Zornberg, *Moses*, 192.

17. Martin Luther King Jr., *A Testament of Hope: The Essential Writings and Speeches of Martin Luther King, Jr.*, ed. James M. Washington (New York: HarperCollins, 1986), 286.

18. Reinhold Niebuhr, *The Irony of American History* (New York: Charles Scribner's Sons, 1952), 63.

Joshua and Samson

1. Shakespeare, *Hamlet*, act 1, scene 3.

2. Taylor Branch, *Parting the Waters: America in the King Years, 1954–63* (New York: Simon and Schuster, 1988), 99.

Priests

1. L. Gregory Jones, *Christian Social Innovation: Renewing Wesleyan Witness* (Nashville: Abingdon Press, 2016), 51.

2. Hugh Heclo, *On Thinking Institutionally* (Boulder, CO: Paradigm, 2008), 98.

3. Ibid.

4. Ibid., 99.

5. Amos Wilder, "Electric Chimes or Rams' Horns," *Grace Confounding* (Philadelphia: Fortress, 1972), 13.

6. Richard D. Nelson, *Raising Up a Faithful Priest: Community and Priesthood in Biblical Theology* (Louisville: Westminster John Knox, 1993), 85.

7. Annie Dillard, *Holy the Firm* (New York: Harper and Row, 1977), 58.

8. Kathleen Norris, *Acedia and Me: A Marriage, Monks, and a Writer's Life* (New York: Riverhead Books, 2008), 187.

9. Gail Godwin, *Father Melancholy's Daughter* (New York: HarperCollins, 1991), 199.

10. Gabriel Barkay, "The Riches of Ketef Hinnom," *Biblical Archaeology Review* 35, no. 4 (July 2009).

11. Meyer, *Setting the Table*, 189.

12. Nelson, *Raising Up a Faithful Priest*, 86.

13. Ibid., 81.

14. Ibid.

15. Mother Teresa, *A Simple Path*, compiled by Lucinda Vardey (New York: Ballantine, 1995), 99.

16. Martin Seligman, *Flourish: A Visionary New Understanding of Happiness and Well-Being* (New York: Free Press, 2011), 33.

17. See the good discussion in Walter Brueggemann, *Finally Comes the Poet: Daring Speech for Proclamation* (Minneapolis: Fortress, 1989), 13–41.

Sages

1. Daniel Goleman, "What Makes a Leader?" *Harvard Business Review*, June 1996.

2. Robert D. Richardson, *Henry Thoreau: A Life of the Mind* (Berkeley: University of California Press, 1988), 282.

3. Aaron Chalmers, *Exploring the Religion of Ancient Israel: Prophet, Priest, Sage and People* (Downers Grove, IL: IVP Academic, 2012), 75.

4. Edwin Friedman, *A Failure of Nerve: Leadership in the Age of the Quick Fix* (New York: Seabury, 2007), 8.

5. Ibid., 13.

6. Collins, *Good to Great*, 73–89.

7. Ibid., 163.

8. Ibid.

Peter and Paul

1. Larry Hurtado, *Why on Earth Did Anyone Become a Christian in the First Three Centuries?* (Milwaukee, WI: Marquette University Press, 2016).

2. Henri Nouwen, *In the Name of Jesus: Reflections on Christian Leadership* (New York: Crossroad, 1989), 17.

3. Ibid., 62.

4. Vanier, *Community and Growth*, 291.

5. N. T. Wright, *Paul and the Faithfulness of God* (Minneapolis: Fortress, 2013), 453, 568.

6. Goldingay, *Old Testament Theology*, 3:708–11.

7. Andrew Clarke, *A Pauline Theology of Church Leadership* (London: T&T Clark, 2008), 126.

8. Dietrich Bonhoeffer, *Letters and Papers from Prison*, ed. Eberhard Bethge (New York: Macmillan, 1971), 360.

9. Jürgen Moltmann, *The Crucified God*, trans. R. A. Wilson, John Bowden (London: SCM, 1974), 223.

10. Michael P. Knowles, *We Preach Not Ourselves: Paul on Proclamation* (Grand Rapids: Brazos, 2008), 265.

Epilogue

1. Bonhoeffer, *Letters and Papers from Prison*, 360.

2. W. H. Vanstone, *The Stature of Waiting* (London: Darton, Longman, and Todd, 1982), 55.

3. Robert Greenleaf, *Servant Leadership: A Journey into the Nature of Legitimate Power and Greatness* (New York: Paulist, 1977).

4. Pollock, *Hudson Taylor and Maria*, 125.

5. My translations—summarizing two approaches various translators take.

6. Michael J. Gorman, *Inhabiting the Cruciform God: Kenosis, Justification, and Theosis in Paul's Narrative Soteriology* (Grand Rapids: Eerdmans, 2009), 33; putting a lovely twist on Ernst Käsemann's famous thought that the cross was "the signature of the Risen One."

7. Andy Crouch, *Strong and Weak: Embracing a Life of Love, Risk and True Flourishing* (Downers Grove, IL: IVP, 2016), 122, 130.

INDEX OF NAMES

Abernathy, Ralph, 53
Aharoni, Yohanan, 104
Andromache, 72

Balthasar, Hans Urs von, 3, 9
Barron, Robert, 37–38, 39
Barth, Karl, xiv
Becket, Thomas, 33
Bennis, Warren, 78
Berry, Wendell, 13
Birch, Bruce, 31
Bismarck, Otto von, 19
Bonhoeffer, Dietrich, 9, 128, 130
Brown, Brené, xiv
Brown, Robert McAfee, 89–90
Brueggemann, Walter, 32, 51, 112, 119
Buber, Martin, 96
Burnham, Daniel, 83–84
Bush, George W., 23

Calvin, John, 53
Chalmers, Aaron, 115
Chamberlain, Neville, 23
Churchill, Winston, 23, 63, 94
Clarke, Andrew, 127
Clines, David J. A., 48
Collins, Jim, 4, 37, 63, 75, 97, 98, 118
Crouch, Andy, 132

Darwin, Charles, 82
Drucker, Peter, xiii, 31, 33

Emerson, Ralph Waldo, 115

Francis of Assisi, 7, 24, 27, 32, 40
Francis, Pope, 13, 27, 33, 89
Frankfurt, Harry, 66
Friedman, Edwin, xiii, 117–18

Gandhi, Mohandas, 23
George, Bill, xii
Ghaemi, Nassir, 23
Gladwell, Malcolm, 29–30
Godwin, Gail, 107–8
Goldingay, John, xi, 51, 70, 78, 79, 126
Goleman, Daniel, 115
Gorman, Michael, 131–32
Greenleaf, Robert, 131
Gunn, David, 22

Hamlet, 72, 101
Heath, Elaine, xii
Heclo, Hugh, 106
Hector, 72
Heifetz, Ronald, xii, 21, 47–48, 50, 86
Henry II, 33
Hitler, Adolf, 23
Hurston, Zora Neale, 96
Hurtado, Larry, 122

Jobs, Steve, 85
Johns, Vernon, 53
Jones, L. Gregory, 105
Jordan, Clarence, 6, 7

Kafka, Franz, 98–99
King, Coretta Scott, 103
King, Martin Luther, Jr., 23, 53, 72, 85, 99, 103
Knowles, Michael, 128–29

Lamott, Anne, 67
Laniak, Tim, 20, 37, 88–89
Laurie, Donald, 50, 86
Leithart, Peter, 67, 68
Lencioni, Patrick, xiv, 36, 67

Levine, Amy-Jill, 5–6
Lewis, John, 53, 94
Lincoln, Abraham, 23, 65
Linsky, Marty, 21
Lowney, Chris, 67
Lundbom, Jack, 72
Luther, Martin, 3, 24, 40, 53, 101

Maimonides, Moses, 56
Mandela, Nelson, 94
Mayer, Diana, xii
McLean, Andrew, xii
Melanchthon, Philip, 53
Meyer, Danny, 4–5, 33, 109
Moltmann, Jürgen, 128
Murphy, Francesca Alan, 27–28, 29
Murphy, Roland, 62, 114, 116

Nelson, Richard, 106–7, 109–10
Niebuhr, Reinhold, 99
Norris, Kathleen, 107
Nouwen, Henri, 13, 79, 123–24

Orpheus, 103

Parks, Lewis, 31
Parks, Rosa, 32, 53, 91
Pierce, Bob, 90
Pollard, Mother, 33, 53

Rad, Gerhard von, 28
Reagan, Ronald, 65
Riva, Vinicio, 33
Rogers, Eugene, 24
Ross, Maggie, 15

Sacks, Jonathan, ix, 56, 60, 82, 83, 91, 95, 98
Scazzero, Peter, 38, 73
Schulz, Charles, 66
Seligman, Martin, 111
Sherman, William, 23
Simeon Stylites, 24
Sims, Peter, xii
Sivers, Derek, 52–53

Taylor, Hudson, 131
Teresa of Avila, 24
Teresa of Calcutta, 57, 110
Thomas, Robert, 78
Thoreau, Henry David, 115
Tolkien, J. R. R., 18, 28, 61
Turner, Ted, 23

Ulysses, 103

Vanier, Jean, 34, 45, 73, 125
Vanstone, W. H., 130

Walzer, Michael, 97
Washington, George, 18
Weaver, Peter, 52
Webber, Andrew Lloyd, 85
Weems, Lovett H., 32
Westermann, Claus, 86–87
Wiesel, Elie, 94
Wilder, Amos, 106
Williams, Rowan, 55–56
Wolpe, David, 37, 38
Wright, N. T., 125
Wyclif, John, 53

Zwingli, Huldrych, 53